DONATED BY
MIKE AND SANDY
COTTER

DECEMBER 1992

THE
NEW
EASTERN
EUROPE

THE NEW EASTERN EUROPE

BY MICHAEL KRONENWETTER

FRANKLIN WATTS
NEW YORK / LONDON / TORONTO / SYDNEY
1991

On the cover: A pro-democracy demonstration
in Prague, Czechoslovakia in November 1989.

Photographs copyright © : Gamma-Liaison: pp. 1 (Patrick Piel), 2 (Eric
Bouvet), 15 top (Leloup/Figaro), 15 bottom (Boleslaw Edelhajt), 16 (Chip
Hires); The Bettmann Archive: pp. 3, 4, 5; UPI/Bettmann Newsphotos:
pp. 6, 9, 10, 12; Franklin D. Roosevelt Library: p. 7 top; AP/Wide World
Photos: pp. 7 bottom, 8; Reuters/Bettmann Newsphotos: pp. 11, 13, 14.

Library of Congress Cataloging-in-Publication Data

Kronenwetter, Michael.
    The new Eastern Europe / by Michael Kronenwetter.
      p. cm.
    Includes bibliographical references and index.
    Summary: Discusses events in Eastern European history which led
    up to the changes and challenges that the region faces today.
    ISBN 0-531-11066-4
      1. Europe, Eastern—History—Juvenile literature. [1. Europe.
    Eastern—History.] I. Title.
    DJK39.5.K76 1991
    940'.09717—dc20   91-18512 CIP AC

CONTENTS

Thursday,
November 9, 1989
11

1
Past Glories
17

2
The Russian Bear
26

3
The End of Empires
38

4
A Brief Moment
of Independence
50

5
An "Iron" Curtain and
a "Cold" War
62

6
"The Breath of Truth"
76

7
The Foundations for Change
85

8
The Peaceful Revolutions
of 1989
96

9
The Bloodbath in the Streets of Romania
112

10
Three Challenges Facing
Eastern Europe
119

11
The Post–Cold War World
129

Source Notes
141

For Further Reading
152

Index
155

THE
NEW
EASTERN
EUROPE

The term "Eastern Europe" refers to the large area in the middle of Europe that fell under the control of the Soviet Union after the Second World War.

It includes the countries of Poland, Czechoslovakia, Hungary, Romania, Bulgaria, and the German Democratic Republic. People sometimes use the term to include Yugoslavia, Albania, and the Baltic republics of the Soviet Union as well. For the purposes of this book, however, we will focus primarily on the six countries listed above.

Eastern Europe as such was a product of Soviet power. Without it, these countries would have continued to go their individual ways. It was only the domination of the Soviets that brought them together and made them into a single political, economic, and military bloc. This is the story of how that bloc was formed—and how it fell apart.

THURSDAY, NOVEMBER 9, 1989

It was the wildest day the divided city of Berlin had ever seen. People flooded into the roadways of both East and West Berlin. Friends embraced ecstatically. Strangers grinned at each other in the streets, sharing a sense of joy and wonder.

As though pulled by a magnet, most of the people were heading toward the Berlin Wall—the great concrete-and-barbed-wire scar that snaked through their city, cutting it in two. People on both sides of the Wall hardly dared believe what they were hearing.

The wall is coming down!
At last.

The Berlin Wall had gone up twenty-eight years earlier, in August 1961. It had been built by the government of East Germany under orders from the Soviet Union.

At that time, the city of Berlin, like Germany itself, had already been divided for years. The division had come about at the end of World War II, a war Germany had started and then lost to the allied nations of the United States, the Soviet Union, Great Britain, and France.

The Allies occupied Germany after the war. By keeping their troops on German soil, they hoped to make sure that Germany could never again become strong enough to start another war. For the same reason, they divided the defeated country in two. The eastern part was left under the control of the Communist USSR; the western part was controlled by the other, non-Communist allies.

The Soviets established a Communist-led government in the east and called the country the German Democratic Republic, or GDR. In the west, the Allies established a capitalist democracy called the German Federal Republic. More commonly, the two new countries came to be known simply as East Germany and West Germany.

The old German capital city of Berlin was inside East Germany. But because of its political importance, the Allies insisted on keeping control of a large section of it, which they called West Berlin. The East Germans resented this. They felt the entire city should have been theirs. Even so, they made East Berlin the capital of the GDR. West Germany made Bonn, which was well inside West German territory, its capital.

In the years that followed, West Germany prospered. East Germany, although it did better than some of its eastern neighbors, seemed to be trapped in an economic mudhole. This contrast was partly due to the difference in the two countries' economic systems: capitalism in the west and communism in the east. But it was also partly due to the different ways the two Germanies were treated by their sponsors. The United States poured all kinds of aid into

West Germany, while the Soviet Union at first seemed determined to punish the people of East Germany for the Nazis' crimes.

Nowhere was the difference in prosperity more obvious than in Berlin. The city had been badly damaged during the war, but West Berlin was quickly rebuilt into a showcase, a thriving Western metropolis. More than a decade after the war, however, East Berlin remained a war-scarred urban wasteland.

It wasn't surprising, then, that many East Berliners envied their neighbors in the West, who were not only wealthier but were politically free. East Berliners began crossing over into West Berlin in great numbers. By August 1961, 2,000 East Germans were emigrating (leaving their country) every day. Berlin was like an open wound, draining East Germany of its talent and self-respect.

The East German government was both saddened and angered by the loss of its citizens. Many of those who were leaving were among the most skilled and educated people in the country. They were the ones with the best chances of finding jobs in the West, but they were also the ones who were most needed at home if East Germany was ever going to build a sound economy.

In Moscow, Soviet premier Nikita Khrushchev resented the flow of people to the West for another reason. For the Soviet government, it was a propaganda disaster, a continuing humiliation for the Communist state the Soviets had established in East Germany. In the eyes of the world, the steady flow of refugees made capitalism and Western-style democracy look increasingly desirable.

That was why Khrushchev ordered the East Germans to build a wall along the border between the two Berlins. The wall went up overnight, taking everyone, including the U.S. government, by surprise.[1]

It began in a makeshift fashion, slapped together from whatever materials the authorities could find. In time, it became a stable, ten-foot-high, concrete-and-barbed-wire structure. It sliced through the city, cutting off east from west, parents from their children, the free from the captive.

Armed guards were stationed in towers along the wall, and it was patrolled by police with automatic rifles, leading attack dogs. The guards were ordered to stop unauthorized people from crossing into West Berlin. They could, and did, shoot people who attempted to escape. During the twenty-eight years of the wall's existence, they killed many would-be escapees, almost all of whom were unarmed and defenseless.

From the moment it appeared that August morning, the Berlin Wall was more than a physical structure cutting through the city. It was a symbol of the whole closed border between East and West Germany. It was a concrete reminder of the imprisonment of the people—not just of East Berlin or even of East Germany, but of all of Eastern Europe. It was the symbol of a divided world.

For at the time the wall went up, the world was as bitterly divided as Berlin was. On one side were the Communist nations, led by the Soviet Union. On the other were the Western democracies, led by the United States. The two groups faced each other in belligerent hostility, each armed with enough nuclear weapons to destroy life on earth many times over. For more than forty years, this confrontation was the central political reality of the world.

Throughout the 1960s, 1970s, and 1980s, the Berlin Wall stood as a hated monument to that confrontation.

Now, in late 1989, as suddenly as it had gone up, it was coming down.

14

*　　*　　*

It happened in a single second. At the tick of midnight on November 9, the border was officially opened. Thousands of people were already waiting on both sides of the gate at Checkpoint Charlie, the main border crossing point in Berlin. The first East German to cross into West Berlin that night was a woman named Angelika Wache.[2] She was only the first of hundreds of thousands more who would cross during the next twenty-four hours. Two days later, a million crossed in a single day.[3]

The crowd waiting on the western side of the border welcomed the visitors with champagne and kisses. Many of those who came were offered more: money, free food, a bed to sleep in that night, and even free tickets to a big soccer game scheduled for that weekend in West Berlin.[4] It was only the beginning of a huge and joyous party that would go on for days. It was, a West German radio announcer proclaimed, "Christmas, New Year's, and Easter rolled into one."[5]

"The Wall Is Gone!" screamed the *Berliner Zeitung* headline the next day: "Berlin Is Berlin Again."[6] In fact, the physical wall was still there. But it was no longer a barrier. Now it was a meeting place.

People from both sides of the city gathered at the wall. They climbed up on it and mingled with each other on the top. Only a day earlier, East German police might have shot them for trying such a thing, but now the police just smiled and waved.

People sat on the wall with their legs dangling over the side, chatting with friends and strangers alike. Some walked along it. Others danced and sang. The wall was like a giant stage on which the people of Berlin—*both* Berlins—acted out their new togetherness.

Television carried pictures of all of this around the globe. American network news anchors arrived to do reports from the scene of these historic events. They stood in front of the wall while behind them the people of Berlin swarmed all over it, creating a beautiful visual image of what freedom felt like.

On November 10, East Berlin police began knocking holes in the wall with bulldozers. To East Berliners, it was an unbelievable sight—East German police working to make it *easier* for people to cross into West Berlin!

The end of the Berlin Wall was as symbolic as the wall itself had been. All over Europe, the old order was breaking down. Things were changing faster than anyone could understand. What was going on? How had all of this started? What did it mean? Where would it lead?

These questions are still being asked today. They are the questions we will explore in this book.

1
PAST GLORIES

Each of the countries of Eastern Europe[1] has its own history. Some were independent states a thousand years ago; others are relatively new, formed out of the turmoil of two twentieth-century wars. Some were once great centers of art and culture; some have always been backward, lagging behind most of their neighbors in matters of learning and the arts. Some have been military powers, gobbling up their weaker neighbors whenever possible; others have spent almost all of their histories trembling in fear of their stronger neighbors.

THE TRIBES

A thousand years ago, what is now Eastern Europe was the constantly shifting domain of many different peoples, or tribes. Important among them were the Magyars and the many Slavic tribes, including the Czechs, the Slovaks, the Bulgars, and the Serbs. It was only gradually, over the centuries, that they began to settle down, with particular branches of particular tribes taking up residence in particular places. Finally, recognizable nations, in the modern sense of the word, began to form.

Even then, the borders of these nations kept changing, as one country after another began to engulf its neighbors. Inevitably, branches of more than one tribe were caught inside the new borders. Most often, one of them would come to dominate all of the others, causing tension and hostility. Eventually, violence and rebellion would break out, and then the borders would shift again.

The tribal origins of the nations of Eastern Europe are far in the past, but they are not buried there. They are vitally important to the present. What began as tribal hostilities a thousand years ago are still reflected in the ethnic hostilities that cause tensions, resentments, and sometimes violence in the nations that exist there today.

Many of these ancient ethnic groups can look back to days of distant glory, days when their ancestors controlled large empires and dominated the other tribes around them. They can also look back to days when their ancestors were dominated, even persecuted, by other tribes. Some reflection of these old glories and old injustices remains.

THE MORAVIAN EMPIRE

One of the first great empires in the region was founded by the Czechs, a Slavic people who lived in Moravia in the ninth century. At its height, the Great Moravian Empire included the neighboring lands of Bohemia to the north and Slovakia to the south, as well as Silesia and parts of what are now southern Poland and northern Hungary.

Moravia's grip on its empire was broken in A.D. 906, when the region was invaded by the Magyars, a tribe of warriors who swept into Europe from the east. Not until the twentieth century would much of the old Moravian Empire be re-formed as the modern nation of Czechoslovakia.

THE BULGARIAN EMPIRES

Meanwhile, Bulgaria was emerging as an important power in south central Europe. Its inhabitants were a blend of Slavs and the descendants of the Bulgars, a Turkish-speaking people who had moved into the region two centuries earlier. Under a czar (or ruler) named Simeon I (A.D. 893–927), Bulgaria subdued the Magyars and conquered neighboring Serbia. For a brief moment, it was the strongest power in the whole area. Modern-day Bulgarian history books claim that this first Bulgarian empire extended as far east as the Black Sea, as far west as the Adriatic Sea, and as far south as the Aegean Sea.[2] Among the lands it controlled was much of what is now Romania.

But this great empire was short-lived. The Russians invaded it in the tenth century and took the Bulgarian capital. They were soon driven out by the forces of the mighty Byzantine Empire, but this did nothing to restore Bulgarian power. Russian rule was simply replaced by the rule of Byzantium.

The Bulgarians rose up against the Byzantine Empire in 1185. Under the Bulgarian czar Ivan I, and later under his son, Czar Kaloyan, a second Bulgarian Empire was formed. At its height in the thirteenth century, it included all of Macedonia, as well as Albania and parts of Serbia. But in 1330, the empire collapsed. Serbia conquered Macedonia, and the Ottoman Turks, who had already conquered what was left of the Byzantine Empire, moved in to take possession of Bulgaria as well. The Turks would rule Bulgaria until modern times.

MICHAEL THE BRAVE OF ROMANIA

The region that is now Romania was once part of the ancient Roman colony of Dacia. Once the Romans were driven out, the area underwent a bewildering series of invasions by the Huns, the Goths, the Magyars, the Slavs, and the Bulgars. Nonetheless, even while spending generations under the subjugation of this succession of invaders, the people still held on to their essentially Roman language and a sense of their own identity.

Finally, in the thirteenth and fourteenth centuries, they achieved a kind of self-government with the establishment of the principalities of Moldavia and Walachia. These were ruled by local princes, who gave their allegiance to European kings, but who were free to rule inside their own principalities more or less as they saw fit.

The fact that the region was no longer dominated by outsiders did little to end the strife that it had become accustomed to. The local princes continually warred against each other and against the wealthy gentry who controlled the farms that made up the bulk of the principalities' wealth.

To the peasants and other common people, it made very little difference who won any of these battles. They were ground deeper and deeper into poverty whoever won. Each new ruler only seemed more oppressive than the last.

Early in the sixteenth century, Walachia and Moldavia fell to the Turks and became part of the Ottoman Empire. Near the end of the century, a Walachian prince called Michael the Brave briefly united the two principalities and defied the Turks.

Michael may have deserved his courageous nickname, but he might also have been called "the Cruel" or "the Devious." He began his drive for Romanian independence—and personal power—by inviting several prominent Turks to visit his castle. He owed them money, and his guests may have thought he was planning to pay them, but he slaughtered them instead. In 1599, he conquered Transylvania, which bordered Walachia on the north. (Long a province of Hungary, Transylvania had come under Turkish rule in 1526.) Michael then moved on to take Moldavia as well. By 1600, he had united all three principalities under his leadership.

Michael was successful in defying the Turks, but he was not so successful in defying the Hungarians, who resented his high-handed actions in Transylvania. They had him assassinated in 1601. Although the conquest of Transylvania led to Michael's personal downfall, it made him the national hero of Romania. It was his brief union of Walachia, Transylvania, and Moldavia that formed the model for the modern Romanian state.

THE GOLDEN AGE OF HUNGARY

Many of the Magyars, who caused so much trouble for the peoples of Europe for centuries, had settled in Hungary by the tenth century. Using it as their base, they continued to raid westward. Along with Moravia and Bulgaria, Burgundy and even northern Italy fell victim to the Magyars before the forces of the Holy Roman Empire drove them out in 955.

Hungary then became a Christian nation and was quickly welcomed into the mainstream of European affairs. Its first king, Stephen I, who was crowned in 1000, solidified Hungary's place in Christian Europe.

He was later named a saint by the Catholic church.

In the early fourteenth century, King Charles I of Hungary married the sister of the king of Poland. Charles's son, Louis the Great, thus became king of both Hungary and Poland. For a time, the joint kingdom was threatened by Turkish invaders, but they were driven out by forces led by a regent named John Hunyadi. Hunyadi became a great national hero, and his son, Matthias Corvinus, was elected king in 1458.

He proved to be one of the most able European rulers of his age. He fostered learning by founding a university, as well as sending Hungarian students abroad to study. The library he established in the city of Buda rivaled almost any in Europe.

He was also an effective military leader. He formed a standing Hungarian army and used it to win control of Austria from the mighty Hapsburg dynasty. He then moved his capital from Buda to the Austrian city of Vienna and had himself crowned king of Bohemia (although he had to share that title with Ladislaus II). Nonetheless, he did bring Moravia, Silesia, and other Bohemian regions under Hungarian control.

Under Matthias Corvinus, Hungary briefly became the most powerful nation in that part of Europe. But he died without an heir who could hold Hungary together. The Hapsburgs of Austria took over much of it, and the Zapolya family of nobles asserted control in their native region of Transylvania.

Meanwhile, the Turks, whom Hunyadi had chased away some three-quarters of a century earlier, came back. On August 29, 1526, a massive Turkish army led by Suleiman the Magnificent crushed a Hungarian force led by King Louis II near the town of Mohács in southern Hungary. King Louis was killed, and Hungary fell under the domination of the Ottoman Empire. The Turks would not be driven out again for more than 170 years, and Hungary would never regain its position of independent power and influence in Europe. By the Peace of Kalowitz (1699), all of Hungary (including Transylvania) was given to Austria.[3] Hungary's golden age was over.[4]

THE FEDERATION OF POLAND-LITHUANIA

In 1386, Queen Jadwiga of Poland married Grand Duke Jagiello of Lithuania. It was a political as well as a romantic union. Jagiello was crowned King Wladyslaw II of Poland, and he and his bride proceeded to found a dynasty that would rule both Poland and Lithuania for the next two centuries.

Under the Jagiellonian dynasty, the federation of Poland-Lithuania became both a great military power and a center of learning and culture. By defeating the Teutonic Knights, it managed to gain control of Prussia and Livonia. It was Poland-Lithuania that spread the cultural developments of the Renaissance throughout much of what is now Eastern Europe.[5]

Even after the end of the Jagiellonian dynasty in 1572, Poland remained a force to be reckoned with in Europe. Militarily, it was the strongest nation in the middle of Europe. It was so strong, in fact, that in 1609 King Sigismund III dared to invade Poland's massive neighbor, Russia.

Poland was an old rival of Russia's by that time. It had engaged its neighbor in a series of religious and territorial quarrels that often turned into wars. Now Sigismund thought he saw a chance to conquer the giant to the east once and for all.

At time—known in Russian history as the "time of troubles"—several hostile forces were struggling for control in Russia. Sigismund tried to take advantage of this turmoil by invading the country and proclaiming himself its king. Polish troops actually occupied Moscow before the Russians finally managed to band together long enough to throw them out.

After that, things went badly for Poland-Lithuania, both inside and outside the federation. The various regions within the large federation had always had somewhat different interests, and political and economic divisions began pulling the country apart. As its internal troubles mounted, its strange governmental system—in which any deputy in its legislature, the Diet, could veto any action—made the country all but ungovernable.

Even worse, Sigismund had made the mistake of arousing the Russian bear. Russia was as quick to take advantage of Poland as Poland had been to take advantage of Russia. But Russia was not the only one. Before long, Poland was being attacked from two sides. Swedish troops swept into Poland from the west while Russian troops swept in from the east. By the end of the 1660s, Poland had lost huge chunks of its territory that it would never get back.

Despite the failing Polish fortunes, it was a Pole who would save much of Europe from being overrun by the Ottoman Empire: King John Sobieski led the Christian forces that crushed a Turkish army outside the Austrian (and Hungarian) capital of Vienna on September 12, 1683. It was such a decisive victory that the Turks never seriously threatened to conquer Europe again.[6] But Sobieski's reign, which ended in 1696, turned out to be the last great bright spot in the history of the Polish kingdom.[7]

Many of the tensions and hostilities that are playing themselves out in Eastern Europe today date back to the times discussed in this chapter. The people who live there now are the descendants of the Slavs, the Magyars, the Czechs, the Bulgars, and the rest, who were already struggling for power in the region a thousand years ago.

The old glories still survive in memory. Old dreams of national independence and national power survive as well. So do the old resentments and hatreds. Ethnic animosity (the hostility felt by one racial, cultural, or national group for another) has played a large part in the history of the region, and it still plays a large part today.

For a thousand years, the countries of the region have struggled among themselves for power and supremacy. Over and over again, they have been forced to endure foreign invasions, from the west and from the east. For much of their history, they have been subjected to foreign rule, whether that of their neighbors in Europe or that of the Ottoman Turks, or the Byzantine Empire.

But more and more, over the past few centuries, real power in the region has come to center in a single foreign nation. It is a nation that has dominated the region as no other has done in its long and violent history. That nation, of course, is Russia, and its successor state, the Union of Soviet Socialist Republics.

2
THE RUSSIAN BEAR

Despite their very different pasts, the nations of Eastern Europe have shared a common fact of geography: their nearness to one of the world's largest, most powerful, and most domineering nations - Russia and its successor state, the Union of Soviet Socialist Republics. More than anything else, it is their nearness to this giant that has determined their political and economic development over the past four centuries.

EARLY RUSSIA

Like the United States, the USSR is a federal union; that is, it is made up of separate and partly autonomous (or self-governing) states. In the Soviet Union, these states are known as republics. There are fifteen of them: Armenia, Azerbaijan, Byelorussia, Estonia, Georgia, Kazakh, Kirghiz, Latvia, Lithuania, Moldavia, Russia, Tadzhik, Turkmen, the Ukraine, and Uzbek. But unlike the United States, the Soviet Union has always been dominated by one of its states: Russia.

The traditional symbol for Russia is a bear. A bear is a massive, lumbering animal who overpowers its enemies through sheer size and strength. It is an appropriate symbol for the role Russia has played in the history of eastern Europe. First as the head of an empire and later as the dominant force within the Soviet Union, Russia has held the lesser states around it in fear and often in subjugation.

But Russia was not always the dominant power in Eastern Europe. The first real Russian state wasn't even founded until the ninth century. It had its capital in Kiev and covered a huge expanse of territory, much more than any other country in Europe. It included part of what became the kingdom of Poland, and it extended northward as far as the Baltic Sea. But much of this enormous area was thinly populated, cold, and primitive.

Although Kievan Russia flourished for a while, it never expanded its power very far westward into Europe. It eventually fell prey to invaders from both the west and the east.[1]

In 1223, the Mongols of Genghis Khan invaded Russia, and for centuries afterward, Russia was under the thumb of their Tartar descendants. They demanded, and got, payments of tribute from generation after generation of Russians. At the same time, armies from Poland-Lithuania and other European countries chipped away at Russia from the west. It was as though the Russian bear were hibernating in its cave, afraid to leave because of wolves waiting for it outside.

THE BEAR STIRS

The Russian bear began to wake up during the reign of Ivan the III (called Ivan the Great) in the fifteenth and early sixteenth centuries.

Ivan began as the grand duke of Moscow, but he

wasn't satisfied with being a mere Muscovite prince. He wanted to be an emperor—the Czar of All the Russias. But before he could really deserve that title, he knew that he would have to get rid of the pesky Tartars.

As grand duke, he laid down a direct challenge to the Tartars by refusing to pay tribute to them. It was a daring move. The future of the country, not to mention the future of the grand duke himself, depended on whether or not he could make his refusal stick. Russians had occasionally refused to pay tribute before, and the Tartars had responded swiftly and brutally. No Russian leader had ever been strong enough to get away with defying them.

Russia's future, as well as Ivan's, hung in the balance on a single fateful day in 1480. Ivan's army faced the Tartar forces across the Ugra River. The Russians were camped on one bank, the Tartars on the other.[2] Both sides expected a battle to the death. But then, suddenly, mysteriously, and without any explanation, the Tartar army turned away from the river and went home without a fight.

Having asserted Russian independence, Ivan went on to unite Russia under his own leadership by force of arms. His efforts are generally considered the founding of the modern Russian state.

Even so, Russia stayed a relatively primitive country by European standards. It wasn't until after its victories over Poland and Sweden that Russia really entered into the mainstream of modern European life. That plunge was taken by Czar Peter I, known as Peter the Great, who ruled from 1682 to 1725. It was Peter who turned Russia into a great empire that included parts of both Europe and Asia.

Peter knew that Russia would need European science and technology if it was to become a major power. He brought European technical and scientific experts to Russia and sent Russian students abroad to become experts themselves. He introduced European customs into his court, reformed the Russian army along modern European lines, and built a Russian navy from scratch.[3] In short, he put Russia on the road to becoming one of the great military powers of the world. Again and again over the next several centuries, Russia would use its growing power to exert its dominance over eastern Europe.

CATHERINE THE GREAT EXTENDS RUSSIAN POWER IN EASTERN EUROPE

If Peter was the ruler who solidified European influence in Russia, it was Catherine II who solidified Russian influence in Europe. Catherine herself was a European, a princess from Germany who came to the Russian throne through marriage. In 1745, she married the man who would one day become Czar Peter III. When Peter was murdered within months of coming to the throne in 1762, Catherine took power over Russia herself. She kept it until her death in 1796.

Catherine began her reign as a domestic reformer. She claimed to admire the works of the liberal French thinkers, such as Voltaire and Diderot, and she even introduced some liberal social reforms into Russia. Later in her reign, she introduced some important political reforms as well.

Catherine had many successes in foreign affairs. It was during her reign, for example, that Russia got a permanent port on the Black Sea, which was important for Russia's future as a naval power. But Catherine's greatest foreign policy success was the destruction of Russia's old enemy, Poland.

THE DESTRUCTION OF POLAND

Russia was not the only eighteenth-century power that was worried about Poland. Prussia, which was the leading German state of its time, was also frightened of a possible revival of the once-powerful Polish state. Between them, Catherine and the king of Prussia, Frederick II, conspired to have Stanislaw Poniatowski named King Stanislas II of Poland in 1764.[4] Poniatowski was Polish by birth, but he was also an ex-lover of Catherine's and still very much indebted to her. With him on the throne, Poland would not present a military threat to Russia, and Catherine could expect to have a great influence in Polish affairs in general.

To some extent, this turned out to be true. Many of Stanislas's policies were heavily influenced by Russia, but not all of them. In many important respects, Stanislas turned out to be more devoted to Polish interests than to Catherine. He even went so far as to try to improve relations with France and Austria, two potential enemies of both Russia and Prussia.

Frederick, meanwhile, was as worried about Poland's friendliness to Russia as he was about Poland's overtures to other European states. Even though he had helped to put Stanislas on the throne, he was troubled by the fact that Catherine had more influence with the king than he did. An independent Poland might one day present a danger to Prussia, but a union between Poland and Russia would present an even greater one.

Catherine and Frederick agreed that something more would have to be done to remove the potential threat from Poland. Their solution was to enlist Austria in a scheme to weaken Poland by chopping off large chunks of the country. In 1772, the three stronger countries partitioned the weaker one, drastically reducing its size. Each of them took a slice of Poland for itself. Austria snatched the southwest corner, Prussia took a hunk out of the western end, and Russia carved off a large strip in the east.

Not satisfied with reducing Poland, they went on to destroy it. In two more partitions, in 1793 and 1795, they divided what remained of the country between them. Of the three, Russia got the largest share.

Poland's obliteration was total. The conspirators even agreed among themselves not to use the word "Poland" anymore.[5] For a time, the name completely vanished from the map of Europe.

When the French emperor Napoleon went to war with Austria and Prussia early in the nineteenth century, many Poles fought on the side of the French. In return, they hoped Napoleon would support an independent Poland. But Napoleon made a deal with Czar Alexander I of Russia. Instead of re-creating Poland, the so-called Peace of Tilsit, signed in 1807, established a new entity called the Duchy of Warsaw. Designed to serve as a buffer between Prussia and Russia, it was made up out of part of Prussia's section of what had once been Poland. What was worse, the duchy was deprived of what had been the region's most important city, Danzig, which was removed and set up as a separate political entity.[6]

Napoleon had set out to conquer Europe, and for a time he was almost successful—until he turned on Russia. As able a military leader as he was, he turned out to be no match for the vast Russian distances or the merciless Russian winter. Forced to retreat from Russia, he was soon defeated by the combined forces of Russia, Great Britain, Austria, and Prussia.

The Congress of Vienna, which the victorious powers held in 1814–1815, established still another version of the Polish state. Once again, the new Poland was much smaller than the one that had existed before the partitions. But according to the constitution announced in 1815, it was at least an autonomous, self-governing state, entitled to its own king and government.[7]

Ironically, however, the reality was just the opposite. Instead of granting real independence to Poland, the Congress of Vienna actually took away what little independence the Duchy of Warsaw had been given by Napoleon. The victors made sure that the Polish crown was placed on the head of Czar Alexander I of Russia. Despite its supposed independence, the new Poland would actually be subject to the will of its old enemy, Russia.

THE POLICEMAN OF EUROPE

There was a reason for the Russian czar's being named king of Poland. By 1815, a new political reality had been established in Eastern Europe. It was clear to everyone now that Russia was a major power in the region. By playing the leading role in the defeat of Napoleon, it had won a place as an equal of the greatest powers in Europe.

Despite its new role, Russia was a conservative nation. It feared change. For most of the nineteenth and early twentieth centuries, Russia used its new power to do battle against political and social change, particularly the kind of change that had erupted in France in the revolution of 1789. Its efforts to put down the forces of revolt whenever they popped up in Eastern Europe earned it the title of "the policeman of Europe."

And in the mid-nineteenth century, revolutionary change was threatening to break out everywhere. All across the continent, liberals and radicals alike were chafing under the rule of oppressive governments. Pressure for change became so great that in 1830 it erupted into actual revolutions in France, Belgium, and Poland.

Czar Nicholas I of Russia left it to others to put down the rebellions in western Europe, but he moved decisively to crush the revolt in Poland. In his role as

Poland's king, he threw out the Polish constitution, abolished the nation's legislature, and even closed the University of Warsaw.

As it turned out, the upheavals of 1830 were only a rehearsal for a much larger outbreak of revolutions that swept Europe in 1848. Although there was no revolution inside Russia itself, Czar Nicholas watched the rebellions elsewhere with real shock and horror. All of his instincts were to restore order, to use Russia's growing power to protect not only his own interests but the interests of the other European monarchs as well. At his direction, Russia took the lead in crushing the revolutions in Eastern Europe.

SUBDUING HUNGARY

Russia was the only major country on the entire European continent that did not suffer from some form of revolution in 1848. Her neighbor and ally, Austria, was not so lucky. By March 1848, the revolutionary fever was raging throughout the entire Austrian Empire.

The infection was strongest of all in Hungary, particularly among the descendants of the ancient Magyars. The Magyars were a privileged class among the Hungarians. They thought of themselves, in fact, as the only true Hungarians. And by the middle of the nineteenth century, this feeling had developed into a fierce sense of Hungarian nationalism. More and more restless under the rule of the Hapsburg dynasty, the Magyars had long been demanding greater autonomy (self-government) from Austria.

Distracted by troubles elsewhere in the empire, the Hapsburg government tried to appease the nationalist sentiment in Hungary. On March 17, 1848, Austria allowed the appointment of Lajos Batthyany as Hungary's first prime minister, an office that would answer to a representative Hungarian Parliament.[8] Hungary's first truly independent parliament met on April 7 and immediately began pressing for even greater independence.[9]

Losing patience, Austria sent troops into Hungary, expecting a quick and easy victory. But the Hungarians, under the leadership of Lajos Kossuth and General Arthur Gorgey, were surprisingly successful in withstanding the onslaught. Then, on April 14, 1849, the Hungarian Parliament made a daring move: it removed the Hapsburg emperor, Franz Joseph I, from the throne of Hungary.[10] This was the ultimate challenge to the young emperor, who had just risen to the throne at the age of eighteen.

Unable to defeat the rebellious Hungarians by himself, Franz Joseph appealed to Czar Nicholas I of Russia. Nicholas was more than willing to help. He moved 150,000 Russian troops from Poland, which had already been subdued in 1830, into Hungary.[11] This massive force was more than a match for the outnumbered and outequipped Hungarians. All resistance was crushed by August 1849, and the leaders of the Hungarian rebellion were executed the following October.

AUSTRIA-HUNGARY

Austria eventually gave Hungary its independence in 1867. The two states then joined in a partial union, known as the dual monarchy of Austria-Hungary, under the Hapsburg crown. Although each of the countries remained self-governing inside its own borders, they acted together in most foreign policy and military matters.

During its short history, which lasted only until the end of World War I, Austria-Hungary was a major power. Its culture was second to few countries anywhere, and its armies were among the most powerful in Europe. In Eastern Europe, it had no real rival except Russia.

Ultimately, however, Austria-Hungary's existence would be imperiled not by war with its mighty neighbor but by a squabble with the relatively insignificant Eastern European nation of Serbia. As we will see in the next chapter, this apparently minor quarrel would have disastrous consequences, not just for Austria-Hungary, Russia, and Eastern Europe, but for the entire world.

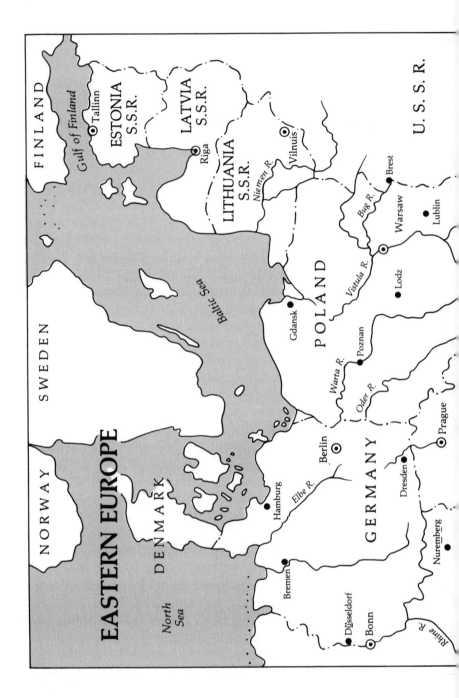

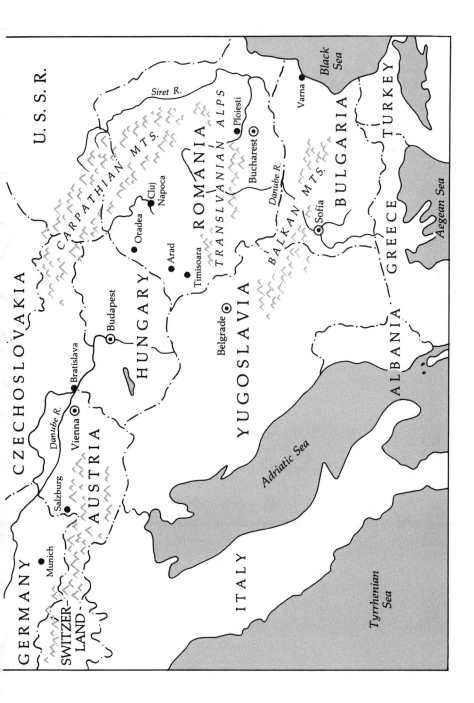

3
THE END OF EMPIRES

By the end of the nineteenth century, the czar of Russia ruled the most massive empire in the world.

In the north, it bordered on the frozen expanse of the Arctic Ocean; in the south, on the smaller but still vast empires of the Ottoman Turks and the Chinese. From west to east, it occupied a huge mass of land between Europe and the Pacific Ocean. Although Russia was thought of primarily as a European power, its Ussuri District actually bordered the great Asian empire of China on the east.

When Czar Nicholas II was crowned on May 26, 1894, he became not just the Emperor and Autocrat of All the Russias but the czar, prince, or grand duke of a variety of other countries, districts, provinces, and regions as well. Among them were the Eastern European lands of Poland and Bulgaria.

He would be the last czar to rule this massive empire. Along with the Austro-Hungarian and Ottoman empires, it would come to a violent end in the most destructive war known to history up to that time, a war caused by the historic conflicts between the ethnic groups of Eastern Europe.

THE BALKANS

World War I began in that part of Eastern Europe known as the Balkans. The Balkan Peninsula thrusts down from the bottom of Europe toward the Mediterranean Sea. It is bounded on the west by the Adriatic and Ionian seas and on the east by the Black and Aegean seas. Its southern end is occupied by the ancient nation of Greece, which some historians consider the birthplace of Western civilization.

Today the northern part of the Balkan Peninsula is occupied by the nations of Bulgaria, Romania, Yugoslavia, and Albania. But in 1914, when World War I began, Yugoslavia did not yet exist. Some of what is now its territory was taken up by the independent nation of Montenegro, some by the semi-independent Hungarian crownland of Croatia, and some by the Austrian provinces of Herzegovina and Bosnia. The rest was taken up by the Slavic nation of Serbia.

Serbia had its eye on Bosnia, a province that was populated mostly by Slavs. Although less than half of the Bosnians were actually Serbs, most spoke the Serbian language and thought of themselves as more or less Serbian. It seemed natural, then, both to the Serbs and to most Bosnians, that Bosnia should become a part of Serbia. This ambition was fully supported by Russia, which considered itself a friend and protector of Serbia.

But Bosnia's situation was complicated. It had been part of the Ottoman Empire for centuries and still legally belonged to the Turks. What is more, it had been put under *Austrian* protection by the Congress of Berlin in 1878, and Austria-Hungary had no intention of giving it up. This was made clear when Austria annexed Bosnia in 1908. The annexation outraged not only the Serbs and the Russians but also many of the Slavs who made up the majority of the population of the entire peninsula.

The Slavs were tired of being ruled by foreign empires. The Austrians and the Magyar Hungarians ruled some of them from the north, and the Ottoman Turks ruled others in the south. A feeling was spreading throughout the peninsula that it was time for the Slavs to unite and free themselves from *all* outside forces.

But the Balkan nations had always been quarrelsome, even with their Slavic neighbors. Bulgaria in particular had a history of feuding with the other Balkan states. Even so, Serbia, Bulgaria, Montenegro, and Greece managed to unite long enough to declare war on a weakened Turkey. They drove the Turks out of all but the southeastern tip of the Balkan Peninsula. But then the Balkan states returned to their quarrelsome habits. Instead of enjoying their joint victory, they began fighting among themselves over the territory they had won.

The so-called Balkan Wars came to an end in 1913, but none of the combatants was particularly happy about the peace settlement. The Bulgarians and Serbians were particularly dissatisfied. Each was convinced it should have gotten more territory from the war.[1]

Despite the fighting among themselves, the Slavs did not forget their mutual grudge against Austria. A seed had been planted that would lead to a much bigger war the very next year. On June 28, 1914, the Archduke Francis Ferdinand of Austria and his wife were paying a visit to Sarajevo, the capital city of Bosnia. The archduke was an important figure, the heir to the Austro-Hungarian throne. While he and his wife were riding through the streets of Sarajevo in a carriage, a man with a pistol stepped forward from the crowd. He fired twice into the carriage, killing not only the archduke but his wife as well.

The assassin was a nineteen-year-old Serbian Slav. There was no real proof that he was anything but a lone assassin, but the Austrian government insisted that the killing must have been ordered by the Serbian government. In fact, later evidence suggested that the murder had been planned by Serbian military intelligence.[2]

In any case, whether Serbia had been directly involved or not, Austria-Hungary decided that it was time to put an end to the Serbian agitation against the empire. It issued an ultimatum to Serbia. Serbia tried to avoid war with a mild response, but Austria-Hungary was determined to fight. It declared war on Serbia on July 28, 1914, and immediately began shelling the capital city, Belgrade. (Belgrade is now the capital of Yugoslavia.)

Russia was traditionally committed to protect the Slavs who lived in the Balkans. What's more, Czar Nicholas II had personally committed himself to protect little Serbia. In a show of support, Nicholas mobilized some troops along Russia's borders.

The mobilization was not intended as a step toward war. It was meant only to pressure Austria-Hungary into negotiating with Serbia. But Kaiser Wilhelm of Germany, who was allied with Austria-Hungary, was angered by the mobilization. Despite appeals for peace from Nicholas, Wilhelm declared war on Russia on the first of August. The next day, German troops invaded Russia's ally, France. Within weeks, almost all of Europe was at war. World War I had begun.[3]

The two main sides in the war were known as the Allies and the Central Powers. Russia was one of the leading Allies, along with Great Britain and France. Austria-Hungary and Germany were both Central Powers. The smaller countries of the region fell into place behind the major powers. The Balkan states of Serbia, Romania, and Montenegro allied themselves with Russia; Bulgaria sided with Austria-Hungary, which included the area of modern-day Czechoslovakia. What is now Poland was divided between the two sides.

But the Great War, as it came to be called, was not confined to Europe. Before it was over, it had infected nations around the globe, including colonies of the European empires from Africa to the Far East, as well as such distant nations as Japan and the United States. A whole generation of young men from more than a dozen countries was decimated. More than 37.5 million of them were killed or wounded.

Politically, the war redrew the map of the world. The Austro-Hungarian, German, Russian, and Ottoman empires were broken up. Austria-Hungary itself was split in two, and each of its once-mighty partners was reduced to a minor power. Even before the war was over, Russia had suffered a a revolution that overthrew the czar and changed the whole course of twentieth-century history.

THE RUSSIAN REVOLUTION

As a ruler, Nicholas II was a bundle of contradictions. Personally, he was a gentle human being with nothing brutal in his character. And yet he ruled a brutal empire. Emotionally, he had a deep affection for the Russian people. He felt their suffering, and he cared deeply about their welfare. Yet he did little to improve their lot. What is more, he was convinced that he had an absolute, God-given right to rule them as he saw fit. He refused to grant democratic rights even to the Russian nobility.

In foreign affairs, he was the leading voice for peace and reconciliation among the European rulers of his time, but he moved so aggressively in the Far East that he provoked a war with Japan in 1904, which Russia lost. The Russo-Japanese War was more than a shocking and humiliating defeat for Russia at the hands of a much smaller power. It revealed an inner weakness in the Russian Empire and sparked a revolution.

Russian society was becoming restless at all levels. Workers and peasants, who lived in grinding poverty, were hungry for better living and working conditions. At the same time, many Russian nobles and professional people were demanding a greater role in running the country. Both were beginning to demand some kind of democracy for Russia. Nicholas was sadly unable to provide for the needs of the millions of poor peasants and was stubbornly unwilling to yield democratic representation to anyone.

On January 22, 1905, a huge demonstration took place in St. Petersburg. More than 100,000 workers and their families marched to the Winter Palace to present a petition to the czar. (Nicholas was not at the palace at the time, but the crowd didn't know that.) Men, women, and children came from all directions, massing together in greater and greater numbers as they neared the palace. Thousands upon thousands of them came sweeping down the broad boulevards, marching through a swirling snowfall on their way to beg the help and protection of their czar.

It was not a violent or even a particularly angry crowd. In fact, several of them sang "God Save the Czar" as they strolled along. Many among them believed that the czar was simply unaware of their suffering. Once he *knew*, they thought, he would surely take care of them.

But the crowds never reached the Winter Palace. Government troops, apparently alarmed by the massive size of the demonstration, opened fire on them. Hundreds of the demonstrators were killed, and hundreds more were wounded.

"Bloody Sunday," as it became known, was a turning point in Russian history. It led to a year of violence on the part of revolutionaries, met by even greater violence on the part of the government. And for all of this, Czar Nicholas II took the blame. An outraged priest named Father George Gapon, who had led the demonstration in St. Petersburg, called Nicholas the "soul-murderer of the Russian Empire."[4] Before long, the czar was secretly being called "Bloody Nicholas," even by many of the same Russians who had once loved and honored him.

In a desperate attempt to end the rebellion, Nicholas backed down from his uncompromising anti-democratic stand. Facing a general strike in October 1905, he signed what became known as the October Manifesto. It granted the Russian people their first real constitution, certain basic civil rights, and even a representative legislature, known as the Duma. These moves toward democracy and freedom saved the czar's government for the time being. But nothing could save it for long.

If the Russo-Japanese War caused cracks to appear in the czar's armor, World War I smashed that armor to bits. It left him naked and defenseless against his enemies. As it turned out, the worst of those enemies were not the armies of the German and Austro-Hungarian empires but the workers and peasants of his own country.

44

Almost immediately after it began, the war in Europe bogged down into a murderous quagmire. The battle lines moved back and forth, pointlessly, across a relatively small area. Millions of men were dying on both sides with nothing to show for it.

Russia, which had mobilized the most men (15 million), was suffering the highest casualties. Most of the Russian soldiers were peasants. They had no idea why they were being sacrificed to the merciless war machine. But ignorant as they were, they could see that the army they had been drafted into was floundering. They soon lost all faith in their officers and in the government they served. They began to desert in droves. Eventually, Nicholas himself went to the front to command the troops, but nothing helped.

Meanwhile, demands for weapons, ammunition, and other war supplies were putting terrible strains on the Russian economy. It would have been difficult for Russia to meet those demands at the best of times; the absence of 15 million able-bodied men from the labor force made it impossible. The price of food soared as wages dropped. Shortages of goods caused real suffering, particularly in the towns, where people could not grow their own food. Everywhere there was a growing sense of defeat, humiliation, and despair.

Workers in Petrograd (the new name of St. Petersburg) went on strike in the spring of 1917. When the army was ordered to break up their demonstrations on March 12, the soldiers refused to attack their fellow citizens and joined them instead. The government was fast losing control, even of the army.

On the same day, representatives of workers and soldiers held the first meeting of a new Petrograd Soviet (or council). Other revolutionary soviets quickly sprang up in cities around the the country.

45

Before long, they were established as the basis of a revolutionary government, led by the Petrograd Soviet.

Meanwhile, the government of the czar simply collapsed. The people didn't want it, and the army wouldn't defend it. The czar abdicated (gave up his throne) on March 15. He and his family retired to their country estate, Tsarskoye Selo. They hardly seemed to matter anymore. A formal Provisional Government was soon established, with Prince Georgi Lvov at its head, but the soviets still held the real power in the country. They ordered Lvov's government to take the czar and his family prisoner, and it did.[5]

By midsummer, a new coalition government had been formed. It was headed by a bright young leader of the Socialist Revolutionary party named Alexander Kerensky. Kerensky's government was essentially socialist and liberal. Its aim was to provide greater freedom for the people of Russia.

The Kerensky government faced a series of daunting challenges. It had to invent a whole new form of government for the country; it had to win the support of people throughout the vast and troubled empire; it had to continue fighting an unpopular war against the Central Powers; *and* it had to restore Russia's devastated economy. What's more, *it had to do all of these things at once!*

While it was trying, a rival group of revolutionaries, known as Bolsheviks, gained control in many of the soviets, including the vitally important Petrograd Soviet. The Bolsheviks were Marxists; that is, they believed in the economic theories of Karl Marx, a nineteenth-century German thinker whose book *Das Kapital*[6] had laid out the basis for a radical form of socialism.

Marx and the Russian Bolsheviks believed that

the modern economic system known as capitalism exploited (took advantage of) the workers and peasants. Capitalist businessmen and landowners made their profits off the hard work of the proletariat, robbing the workers of the fruits of their labors. According to Marx, the two groups were locked in a death struggle. Inevitably, the Marxists believed, the proletariat was bound to win because of historical forces that were ultimately beyond anyone's control. Whenever historical conditions were right in a particular society, they claimed, the workers would rise up and overthrow the capitalists, taking over the factories and farms for themselves.[7]

The Bolsheviks believed that conditions were right in Russia in 1917, and they were determined to help the inevitable victory along. Taking advantage of the Kerensky government's weakness, the Bolsheviks seized control of the country in October 1917.

An American journalist named John Reed was in Russia at the time of the October revolution. He wrote an eyewitness account that he called *Ten Days That Shook the World*.[8] The title was no exaggeration. The Bolsheviks' victory did indeed shake the world. Eventually, it would also lead to the virtual enslavement of the countries of Eastern Europe—but not right away. At first, in fact, the Bolshevik Revolution was a liberating force in eastern Europe.

THE BREAKUP OF THE RUSSIAN EMPIRE

On November 7, 1917, the Congress of Soviets declared itself to be the true government of Russia. The new government, which was dominated by the Bolsheviks, was led by Vladimir Ilyich Ulyanov, who called himself Lenin. It was far more radical then Kerensky's government had been, and it moved much faster. It quickly opened peace negotiations with Ger-

47

many, resulting in the Treaty of Brest-Litovsk on March 3, 1918.

This treaty not only took Russia out of the war, it called for the breakup of the western part of Russia's empire. Among the territories Russia gave up were Russian Poland (which had been fighting against Russia in the war in any case) and the Baltic states of Estonia, Latvia, and Lithuania.

Lenin's government was not deeply concerned about losing these foreign territories. It claimed that it was not interested in borders, only in the cause of the workers' struggle against capitalism everywhere. It predicted that workers' revolutions would soon break out all over Europe. In the meantime, national borders hardly mattered.

THE FOUNDING OF CZECHOSLOVAKIA AND YUGOSLAVIA

The war that Russia abandoned in 1917 was won by the Allies the following year. In the peace negotiations that followed in Paris, several Eastern European peoples clamored for their freedom from the defeated Austro-Hungarian and German empires.

Among them were the Czechs and the Slovaks, two neighboring Slavic peoples who had been chafing under the rule of the Austro-Hungarian Empire. The Czechs, who lived mostly in the Austrian provinces of Bohemia and Moravia, had been under the domination of Austria for several centuries. The Slovaks had been subjects of Magyar-ruled Hungary for a thousand years. But now that Austria-Hungary was losing the war, they sensed a chance for independence at last.

On October 28, 1918, a "national council" representing both Czechs and Slovaks met in Prague, Bohemia, to declare the founding of "The Independent

Czecho-slovak State."[9] The war ended the very next month. Encouraged by U.S. president Woodrow Wilson, the victors at the peace conference recognized Czecho-slovakia as a victorious ally. The territory of the new nation was carved out of the northern reaches of the defeated Austro-Hungarian Empire. It included the states of Bohemia and Slovakia, as well as parts of Ruthenia and Silesia.

The government established in the new state was a parliamentary, Western-style democracy. Its first president was Tomáš Masaryk, a Czech who had won President Wilson's support for Czechoslovakian independence during the war.

While the Slavs in northern Austria-Hungary were busy forming Czechoslovakia, the Slavs in the south were pressing for a state of their own. The same month that Czechs and Slovaks met in Prague, representatives of Slavs from Hungarian-dominated Croatia and Austrian-dominated Slovenia met in Zagreb, Croatia. They called for a union with Serbia. Montenegro joined in the call soon after. On December 1, 1918, King Peter I of Serbia accepted the crown of the new nation, which was dubbed the Kingdom of the Serbs, Croats, and Slovenes. His son, Alexander, became king two years later. The country was renamed Yugoslavia in 1929.

The new state included both Serbia and the prewar Austrian province of Bosnia. Gavrilo Princip, the Serbian assassin who had set off World War I, had accomplished his goal.

4
A BRIEF MOMENT OF INDEPENDENCE

Russia's withdrawal from World War I did not mean an end to the suffering and death in Russia. Counterrevolutionaries launched a bloody civil war against the Bolsheviks. To discourage the counterrevolutionaries, the czar and his entire family were killed.[1] The Bolsheviks—who renamed themselves the Communist party—won the civil war. In 1924, they re-formed what was left of the Russian Empire into a federation called the Union of Soviet Socialist Republics.

Although each of the so-called republics had a certain amount of autonomy within its own borders, the federation as a whole was run, often ruthlessly, from the Kremlin in Moscow. After Lenin's death, Joseph Stalin ruled the Soviet Union as a virtual dictator until his death in 1953.

The Communist government had set itself an incredibly ambitious task. It had to establish more than a new governmental system for one of the largest and most diverse countries on earth. It had to invent a new economic system and even a new society as well.

In trying to achieve all of this, the Communists under Stalin were as brutal and as merciless as any of the Russian czars had been.

In a series of five-year plans, the Soviet economy was forced into the industrial age. Industries and farmlands were nationalized (taken over by the government). A massive program was launched to "collectivize" all of the nation's farms under government control. Millions of peasants, who had hoped to own their own land after the revolution, rebelled. But anyone who stood in the way of the Communists' plans was crushed. It is said that as many as 7 million peasants died, millions of them in the mass starvation that resulted from the chaos on the farms and millions more from mistreatment in government forced-labor camps.

Busy reforming its own society, the Soviet Union had little time for trying to gain (or regain) control over the nations of Eastern Europe. Meanwhile, the other great empires that had competed for domination of Eastern Europe had been destroyed by the war.

For a rare moment in history—roughly two decades between the end of World War I and the beginning of World War II—most of the nations of Eastern Europe were independent. For that brief moment, they were free to run their own affairs as they saw fit.

Unfortunately, few of these experiments in independence were successful. In country after country, attempts to bring about social justice foundered on the rocks of ethnic hostilities and tension. Economic reforms failed. Attempts to establish workable democratic governments collapsed. One after another, most of the countries in the region fell under the whips of authoritarian regimes, some of the right and some of the left.

HUNGARY

Cut loose from Austria and from its own empire, Hungary bounced wildly from one kind of government to another. In January 1919, the country proclaimed itself a republic, with Count Mihály Károlyi as president. Karolyi was a liberal. He wanted to find a middle ground between Hungary's conservative large landowners, on the one hand, and its Bolsheviks, who wanted to establish a Soviet-style state, on the other. But neither of these extreme groups was willing to compromise, and Károlyi's regime collapsed in March. The Hungarian government was turned over to a Communist journalist named Belá Kun.

Kun became a dictator, launching what his enemies called a Red (that is, Communist) Terror in Hungary. He set out to imitate the Soviet Union by nationalizing large farms, banks, and other major industries. Unwilling to accept the loss of Slovakia to the new nation of Czechoslovakia, Kun tried to reclaim Hungary's old territory. He even sent a Hungarian army into Slovakia, but it was forced by the Allies to withdraw. Following this defeat, Kun was faced with a counterrevolution inside Hungary itself. When Romania invaded on the side of the counterrevolutionaries, Kun fled the country.

Hungary had swung from liberalism to communism in just a few months' time. Now it swung again, this time to the conservative right. A new government, led by Admiral Miklós Horthy, presided over a "White Terror." The Communist party was outlawed, anti-Semitism was encouraged, and for the next twenty years Hungary moved backward, into the past. For most of that time, national policy was determined largely by the Magyar landowners who had run the country during the nineteenth century.[2]

POLAND

Poland proclaimed itself a republic in November 1918. For the next few years, it had a democratic government that, among other things, launched a major land reform program to spread farm ownership among the peasants. But Poland was not just the largest of the eastern European countries, it was also the most diverse. With several million Ukranians, some 3 million Jews, and over a million Byelorussians, among its other minorities, it suffered from constant tensions between the different ethnic groups and between them and the majority Poles. Rule by democratic government proved to be messy and not very efficient.

In 1926, a coup led by Marshal Jozef Pilsudski toppled Poland's democratic government. Pilsudski was a onetime Socialist who had been a national hero in the struggle for Polish independence against Russia and Germany. But now he turned out to be an intensely authoritarian ruler. Within a few years, he had established what amounted to personal control of the government of Poland. He exercised this virtual dictatorship until 1935, when the government was partially liberalized.[3]

BULGARIA

The most unusual of all the postwar Eastern European governments came to power in Bulgaria in 1919. It was led by Alexander Stamboliski, the radical leader of Bulgaria's Agrarian Union. Supported by the Orange Guard, a group of peasants like himself who enforced his policies with clubs, Stamboliski also established a dictatorship. Unlike most of the other dictatorships in Eastern Europe, Stamboliski's regime seemed to be sincerely devoted to the interests of the peasants. His dream was to found a "Green International" that would unite the governments of all of the neighboring states on behalf of the peasants.[4]

This unique experiment came to a violent end in 1923, when Stamboliski was overthrown and killed. A new government tried but failed to reconcile the interests of several different Bulgarian political parties. In the ten years after Stamboliski's death, there were 864 political assassinations in the country.[5] This chaos was followed by an invasion from Greece in 1934. King Boris III took power in a coup later in the year. One year later, he made himself dictator.

ROMANIA

Romania came out of World War I about twice as big as it had been when the war started. It picked up a large amount of territory (including disputed Transylvania) from the breakup of the Austro-Hungarian Empire; and from Russia, it gained Bessarabia. This expansion was welcomed as a great achievement by the Romanian government, but it presented the country with a problem that would haunt it in the future: large new minority populations, particularly of Transylvanians and Hungarians.

Until 1928, Romania's government was under the control of Ion Bratianu. Although the head of the Liberal party, Bratianu was a very authoritarian ruler. Among his government's measures was a policy of "Romanization," which involved nationalizing or redistributing all of the lands and businesses in Romania that had belonged to foreigners or to Romanian Jews.[6]

Bratianu was replaced in 1928 by a National Peasants party government, which started to carry out land reforms. In 1930, it invited the exiled Crown Prince Carol to return to the country and share political power as King Carol II.

By then, however, the Great Depression was sweeping the Western world. It hit Romania, which had never been prosperous even in the best of times, particularly hard. Along with even greater poverty and suffering, the Depression brought political turmoil. The 1930s saw ferocious outbursts of anti-Semitism and the rise of a fascist, Nazi-like party called the Iron Guard. Strict censorship and anti-Jewish laws were put into effect. King Carol took dictatorial powers in 1938.

CZECHOSLOVAKIA

As we have seen, most of the countries of Eastern Europe did not adjust well to independence. By the late 1930s, Poland, Hungary, Bulgaria, and Romania had all fallen under the iron fist of dictatorial regimes. The same was true of nearby Yugoslavia; and in Germany, the Nazi dictator Adolf Hitler had come to power.

But there was one exception to this dismal record: Czechoslovakia, which proved to be the great success story of Eastern Europe between the wars. Alone among the states of the region, it managed to establish a free, democratic, and workable independent state.

Czechoslovakia began with an advantage over most of its neighbors. Its economy was in good shape, thanks largely to the solid industrial base that had been built in its cities during the days of the Austro-Hungarian Empire. The new government supported this base with a revolution of sorts in the countryside, handing over much of the land that had belonged to wealthy Austrians in the days of the empire to the local peasants.

But the real key to Czechoslovakia's success was the fact that its government worked. The government of the First Republic, as it came to be known, was based largely on the French and American democratic systems. It provided Czechoslovakia with by far the most stable government in the region. In addition, Czechoslovakia had the advantage of excellent leadership from Tomáš Masaryk and Eduard Beneš,[7] who were its only two presidents during the two decades between the wars. They managed to put together a series of effective coalitions, made up of several different political parties, and make them work together to run the country.

This doesn't mean that Czechoslovakia escaped all of the problems that plagued the rest of Eastern Europe. Like its neighbors, Czechoslovakia had to deal with serious divisions between its ethnic groups. But although the minority Slovaks resented the greater power of the Czechs, the two groups were usually able to compromise their differences in ways that ethnic groups elsewhere in the region were rarely able to do.

WARNINGS OF WAR

Independence for the countries of Eastern Europe was born in World War I and died in World War II. People were already worried that another war was coming by the mid-1930s. The main reason for their fears was the aggressive attitude of Adolf Hitler, the head of the National Socialist (Nazi) government of Germany.

Like many other Germans, Hitler had felt humiliated by his country's defeat in World War I, and he was outraged by the treatment it had received from the victors. But Hitler wanted more than revenge for Germany's disgrace. He wanted to return Germany to its past days of empire and military glory. From the time he first came to power in 1933, he'd been pre-

56

paring for an aggressive war, building up German armaments far beyond anything the country needed for its defense.

Hitler moved first against Austria, which had been declared an independent state after World War I. Hitler, who had been born in Austria, insisted that it was historically a German state and belonged in a union with Germany. Ignoring the wishes of the Austrian government, Hitler sent German troops into Austria in 1938. Since Austria had no military defenses to speak of and could offer no resistance, it was quickly absorbed into Nazi Germany.

Some of the other European governments protested, but none took any action against Germany. They justified their lack of action by telling themselves that the Austrians were a German-speaking people and that many Austrians welcomed the union with Germany. Besides, they hoped that Austria would satisfy Hitler's greed for territory. But it didn't. Having taken Austria, he turned his attentions to the neighboring nations of Eastern Europe.

THE FALL OF CZECHOSLOVAKIA

Ironically, the first Eastern European country to lose its independence was the only one that had made a real success of it. Even more ironically, Czechoslovakia had been not only the most stable country in Eastern Europe but also the best defended. Unfortunately, its strongest defenses were in the Sudeten Mountains in the northern and western parts of the country. This was not only the borderland between Czechoslovakia and Germany, it was the home of a large German-speaking minority.

A Czechoslovakian political party made up of ethnic Germans had been campaigning for self-determination and autonomy for the Sudetenland for some time. In September 1938, Hitler announced that Germany supported these demands.

The Czechoslovakian government tried desperately to appease Germany, to give in to enough of its demands to keep it from using force. It had little choice. Czechoslovakia was not strong enough to fight Germany alone, and no other European nation was willing to help. Russia said it might help but only if France helped too, and both France and Britain were pressing for more appeasement. No help could be expected from Czechoslovakia's East European neighbors, Hungary and Poland. Far from helping, they were demanding Czechoslovakian territory for themselves.

In negotiations held in the German city of Munich in late September 1938, Germany, France, Great Britain, and Italy decided that Czechoslovakia should surrender large chunks of its western territory to Germany. Faced with this so-called Munich Agreement, the government of Czechoslovakia gave in. Germany then gave some of the surrendered territory to Hungary. Not wanting to be left out, Poland made its own demands on Czechoslovakia, which gave up still another slice of territory to Poland. As a result of all this, Czechoslovakia lost some of its strongest defenses, as well as almost 5 million of its citizens. The majority of these were ethnic Germans, and some were ethnic Magyars; but about 900,000 of them were Czechs, and another 300,000 were Slovaks.[8]

The Munich Agreement was only the beginning of the destruction of Czechoslovakia. President Beneš fled the country in October, and a right-wing, pro-German government took over. On March 14, 1939, German troops moved across the border, taking the Czechoslovakian capital of Prague the next day. The once-independent democratic nation was split into two puppet states: the Bohemia-Moravia Protectorate and the Protected State of Slovakia.[9] The "protector" in each case was Germany.

Czechoslovakia was the first Eastern European state to lose its independence. The end of independence for others would soon follow.

THE NAZI-SOVIET PACT

Until "the rape of Czechoslovakia," many western European leaders had been unsure about Germany's real aims. Some of them had hoped that Hitler would stop with Austria. For the most part, this was wishful thinking. None of the European leaders (except perhaps Hitler) wanted a war. World War I had been incredibly destructive to all of their countries, and recent advances in military technology assured that another war in Europe would be even worse.

Of all the European leaders, Joseph Stalin was the most frightened of war with Germany. He knew what Hitler's real aims were: Hitler was bent on conquest. And Stalin could read a map. He could see that Hitler was moving east, and that meant toward the Soviet Union. This was particularly frightening to Stalin because he knew that the Soviet Union would never be able to stop the Nazi war machine alone. As Nikita Khrushchev, who would one day rule the Soviet Union himself, later reported, "Stalin had obviously lost all confidence in the ability of our army to put up a fight."[10]

Unable to protect the Soviet Union militarily, Stalin tried to protect it diplomatically. He postponed the German threat by making a friendship agreement with Germany on August 23, 1939. In this so-called Nazi-Soviet Pact, Russia agreed to remain neutral in a fight between Germany and the Western powers. In return, Germany granted the Soviet Union certain useful economic rights.

More important—and more tragically for the future of Eastern Europe—Germany granted Russia a free hand in the three Baltic states of Estonia, Latvia, and Lithuania, and in the eastern half of Poland.

Both Germany and the Soviet Union gained something from the Nazi-Soviet Pact. For Hitler, the pact amounted to a great, bloodless victory. Historically, Germany had always had to worry about fighting its wars on two fronts: battling European armies on the west and Russian armies on the east. Now Hitler's eastern border was buffered (or protected) by the territory Germany had obtained from the Soviet Union.

Just over a month after the pact was signed, Hitler took advantage of it by invading the western half of Poland. As he boasted in a speech to his followers, "What has been . . . considered impossible to achieve has come to pass. For the first time in history we have to fight on only one front."[11] Germany could now concentrate all of its strength in the battle against the Western powers.

For the Soviets, the pact had established a buffer between itself and any sudden attack from Germany. But Stalin was not fooled. He knew that an attack was bound to come eventually, pact or no pact. But at least he had bought time in which to prepare the Soviet military for the battle to come.

For Eastern Europe, however, the Nazi-Soviet Pact was a total disaster. The Germans and the Soviets had decided to protect themselves from each other by taking over the nations of Eastern Europe. Within a month of the German invasion of western Poland, the Soviets moved into Eastern Poland to establish their own buffer there. Soon after that, the Soviet army moved into the Baltic states as well. In 1940, with Soviet troops already in virtual control, each of the three Baltic states was forced to agree to become a constituent republic of the Soviet Union.

A significant portion of Eastern Europe was now under the direct control of the Soviet Union. That control would be temporarily lost in the course of the fighting during World War II. But the Soviet claim had been staked. In the aftermath of the war, the entire region would fall under Soviet domination.

5
AN "IRON" CURTAIN AND A "COLD" WAR

The ex–prime minister of Great Britain, Winston Churchill, came to the United States in 1946 and gave a speech at Westminster College in Fulton, Missouri. The subject of his speech was the spread of Soviet power in Eastern Europe. "From Stettin in the Baltic to Trieste in the Adriatic," he declared, "an iron curtain has descended across the continent."[1]

That "iron curtain" had begun to fall in the early days of World War II, when the Soviet Union first took control of eastern Poland. It continued to fall during and after the war, as the Soviet Union first liberated the countries of Eastern Europe and then took control of them for itself.

TAKING SIDES IN WORLD WAR II

Germany finally attacked the Soviet Union on June 22, 1941, causing Stalin to join the Western Allies. As part of the attack, German troops swept through eastern Poland, driving the Soviets out altogether. A Polish government-in-exile that had already been set up in London called on all Poles to resist the Germans. Many of them did, carrying out guerrilla raids on German troops and communication lines.[2]

Meanwhile, other Eastern European countries were lining up on the side of Germany and the Axis powers. The puppet state the Germans had set up in the Slovak region of captive Czechoslovakia promptly joined the war on the German side. Hungary had also sided with the Germans by signing the so-called Tripartite Pact with the Axis powers on November 20, 1940.[3] Bulgaria joined the following March.

From the start, the Romanian government had done everything it could to appease Germany. It turned over a part of Transylvania to Germany's ally, Hungary, and still other Romanian territory to Bulgaria. It even submitted willingly to occupation by German troops. And finally, King Carol named Ion Antonescu, a pro-Nazi leader of the Nazi-like Iron Guard, to be dictator of the country. Romania formally joined the Axis powers in 1941, and took part in the invasion of the Soviet Union that June.[4]

"TO THE VICTOR BELONG THE SPOILS"

At one time or another during the war, every country in Eastern Europe was either an ally of Germany or under German occupation. Even a large part of the Soviet Union fell under Nazi control. Although some Eastern European businessmen and political leaders benefited under the Nazis, the racial, ethnic, and political minorities in these countries did not. Millions of Jews, Gypsies, Communists, liberals, and Catholics were executed or sent to die slower and more painful deaths in extermination camps.

The Soviets eventually managed to pull their forces together and push the Germans back, not only from Soviet territory but from much of Eastern Europe as well. In 1944, the Soviets had pushed into Poland and the Balkans. The arrival of the Soviets touched off local uprisings against the German occupiers. In Romania, for example, King Michael (who had succeeded King Carol) led a coup that turned the pro-German dictator Antonescu out of office. In Bulgaria, the anti-German revolt was led by a coalition of Bulgarian Communists and Agrarians (a farm-oriented party). In both countries, the new governments joined the Allies and promptly declared war on the Axis powers.

The victorious Soviet troops continued their drive through Eastern Europe. In early 1945, they took Hungary from the Germans. In May, they were the first Allied troops to reach, and therefore capture, the German capital of Berlin.

By May 7, 1945, the day the war in Europe ended, the Soviets were in control of virtually all of eastern Europe. For many of the people of the region, Russia was the liberator that had freed them from the Nazis. This was particularly true of the members of the native Communist movements that had led the resistance against the Nazis in several of the countries. The people's gratitude, along with the presence of Soviet troops, put the Soviet Union in a powerful position to influence events in the area after the war.

There is a cynical axiom of war: "To the victor belong the spoils." For the Soviet Union, the spoils were the nations of Eastern Europe.

The Soviet Union did not take over Eastern Europe the way the old colonial powers had once taken over their colonies. The colonial powers had ruled their empires as exploiters. They considered them as virtual possessions and took every possible economic advantage of them.

The Soviet Union, on the other hand, took over the nations of Eastern Europe as territories within a "sphere of influence." It never actually claimed them, as England had once claimed its colonies in America or as France had claimed its colonies in Indochina. Nor did it take particular advantage of them economically. If anything, it was the other way around, with the Soviet Union propping up the miserable economies of the Eastern European nations.

But the price for Soviet economic and military help turned out to be terribly high. It included the surrender of national independence and the sacrifice of the personal freedoms of the citizens of Eastern Europe.

But if the Soviet Union was not going to exploit the nations of Eastern Europe, why did it want them at all? The main reason was geography. Twice in the twentieth century, the Soviet Union had been invaded from the west, and each time the USSR had been devastated. The Russians had suffered the greatest losses of any country involved in World War I, even though it had pulled out in the middle of the war. And more than 20 million Soviet citizens had died in World War II, 7 million of them civilians! No other nation had ever suffered casualties on such a massive scale.

Still recovering from these terrible losses, Stalin was determined to protect the Soviet Union's western borders at all costs. And that meant using the nations of Eastern Europe as buffers. To Stalin, the independence of the Eastern European nations seemed a small price to pay for Soviet security.

Even the Allies had to recognize the validity of the Soviet's concerns, however unfair they considered its postwar policies to be. And although many politicians in the West called for action to stop the

Soviets, the Allies were faced with the overwhelming military fact that Soviet troops were already in control of Eastern Europe.

DIVIDING UP EUROPE

Even before the war was over, the Big Three nations (Russia, the United States, and Great Britain) met at Yalta in the Soviet Crimea. They agreed that after the war Russia would have possession of some of what had been eastern Poland. In return, Poland would be granted some territory from Germany to help it defend itself from any future German attack.

Not long after the war, in July and August 1945, the Big Three met again, at Potsdam, Germany. This time, they divided defeated Germany into several parts. In line with the Yalta agreement, Poland was given administrative control of the strip of Germany that reached from the prewar Polish border to the Oder and Neisse rivers.

The rest of Germany was split into four "zones of occupation." Each of the Big Three, plus France, took control of a part of the conquered country. Of the four, Russia was granted the biggest zone, consisting of almost all of eastern Germany. The city of Berlin, which was entirely inside the Russian zone, was divided into separate Russian, American, British, and French sectors. In reality, these agreements were only a formal acceptance of what had already happened.

COMMUNIST TAKEOVER

In principle, the Big Three had all agreed to promote democracy in Europe. And in fact, elections were held in each of the Eastern European countries after the war. Most of those elections resulted in coalition governments, made up of representatives of several political parties. Communists were prominent in each of the new governments.

There were several reasons for the Communists' popularity in Eastern Europe. One was the important role (sometimes the most important role) that Communists had played in resisting the Nazis during the war. Another was the fact that the Communists were identified in people's minds with opposition to the big landowners and the tyrannical governments that had dominated most of these countries before the war. Still another reason was the fact that local Communist parties were supported by the Soviets, who were seen by many Eastern Europeans as the liberators who had freed them from the Nazis. (This wasn't true everywhere. It was true in Czechoslovakia, for example, but not in Poland.)[5]

In most of these countries, the Communists moved quickly from being a key part of a coalition government to taking complete control. In Czechoslovakia, for example, the Communists had won more votes than any other party in the postwar election of 1946, but Eduard Beneš was elected president, and Jan Masaryk (Tomáš Masaryk's son) was named foreign minister. Both were liberal Socialists, not Communists. But in 1948, the Communists staged a coup, and before long both Beneš and Masaryk were gone. Beneš resigned in disgust over the constitution the Communists introduced, and Masaryk either jumped or was pushed out of a window.

When the leaders of Poland's wartime government-in-exile returned home, they were frozen out of the postwar government by the Communists. In Bulgaria, the election held in 1946 was so overwhelmingly rigged that the Communists carelessly announced their victory the day before people went to the polls to vote.[6]

In the November 1945 election in Hungary, the

Communist party won only about 22 percent of the vote, giving them less than one-quarter of the seats in the national parliament. Nonetheless, by using a variety of tactics, the Communists soon managed to eliminate all opposition. They chased some anti-Communist leaders out of the country by charging them with conspiring against the government. They pressured their main left-wing rivals, the Social Democrats, to join them in a unified Hungarian Workers party and then simply purged (or removed) the most troublesome of them from the new party. By the time the next elections were held, there was only one slate of candidates on the ballot—those picked by the Communists within the Hungarian Workers' party.[7] A similar, but much more violent, process took place in Romania. In fact, as Paul Landvai wrote in his book *Eagles in Cobwebs*, "The main features of the process . . . were depressingly similar throughout the Soviet orbit."[8]

FOLLOWING THE SOVIET MODEL

The Soviet Union encouraged (and to some extent probably directed) these takeovers of Eastern European governments by the Communists. In some countries, the takeovers actually took place while Soviet troops were still there, with at least the threat of Soviet force to back them up.

The Soviet Union was willing to help for two reasons. The first was self-protection. The second was Communist solidarity. Solidarity—mutual support between people with the same interests and goals—was a basic principle of Communist philosophy. Communists around the world believed that they were engaged in the shared struggle of all workers against their capitalist "masters." They believed that it was their duty to help fellow Communists everywhere.

The Communists of Eastern Europe repaid the Soviet Union by turning their countries into Soviet satellites, looking to the USSR for direction and example. One after another, the new Communist governments declared their countries "soviet republics" or "people's republics," like those of the Soviet Union. Although they held elections, the elections meant little since only one party—the Communists—could run in most of them.

Because Soviet-style communism was antireligion, the Eastern European governments closed down most churches, and priests and ministers were forbidden to conduct services. Those who insisted on carrying on religious activities anyway were usually arrested or sent into exile as enemies of the state.

Economically, too, the satellites tended to follow the Soviet model: nationalizing major industries and collectivizing the farms. Most people worked for the central government. The government planned the economy and told the industries what goods to produce and how much. The basic needs of the people for food, clothing, shelter, education, and health care were taken care of by the government. But the governments could supply only what the inefficient economies could produce. The result was a low standard of living compared to that in the nations of western Europe.

Although all of the Eastern European countries followed the Soviet example to some extent, there were differences between them. Many of these differences had to do with Communist ideology. In some countries, like East Germany, the leaders and much of the population wholeheartedly embraced the principles and beliefs of communism. But in other countries, even some of the leaders who helped impose the Communist system on their people were less than true believers themselves.

In Poland, for example, communism was imposed halfheartedly at best. As the journalist Lawrence Weschler described the result: "There is a large sector that is officially state-owned, a small sector that is officially private, and a remarkably large sector occupying an undefined region between the two."[9] One proof of Poland's lack of real commitment to communism was in the area of agriculture. Poland is an agricultural country—it had once been considered a major "breadbasket of Europe"—so collectivizing the farms should have been the cornerstone of any wholehearted move into communism. And yet most of Poland's farms were never collectivized.

Another key was Poland's attitude toward the Catholic church. Poland was historically a devoutly Catholic country, whereas communism was a rabidly antireligious ideology. Although the Communist government officially discouraged Catholicism and sometimes even persecuted Catholic leaders, the church never ceased being a powerful influence in Polish life.

Large underground economies eventually grew up in countries like Poland and Hungary. Many workers moonlighted, taking second, private jobs that the government either didn't know about or wouldn't tolerate.[10] There was an active black market, where goods of various kinds were traded free of government regulation. But the governments of other countries, like East Germany and Czechoslovakia, refused to tolerate the underground economy and so had less of it.

But even in East Germany, there was some economic experimentation. More and more embarrassed by the prosperity of West Germany, East Germany introduced a "new economic system" in the mid-1960s. Centralization was relaxed, and some industries were permitted to make small profits (although the government insisted that profits be given to the workers or used to improve productivity).

70

The foreign policies of the Eastern European countries were heavily influenced, if not controlled, by the Soviet Union. They voted so often with the Soviet Union in the United Nations that they came to be known as the Soviet, or Eastern, bloc. (A group that usually votes or acts together is called a bloc.)

The level of Soviet control of foreign policy varied from satellite to satellite. By the 1960s, for example, the Romanian dictator, Nicolae Ceaușescu, was steering an almost independent course in foreign policy. But despite such exceptions, there were usually strict limits to how much independence the Soviet Union would tolerate from the Eastern Europeans. As a result, the Soviet bloc stayed remarkably solid from the 1940s until the late 1980s. (There was a great exception in Yugoslavia, whose independent Communist leader, Marshal Tito, broke with Stalin in 1948. Because of this break, Yugoslavia never became a real part of the Eastern bloc, and so we don't deal with it in this book.)

The solidarity of Eastern European Communists with the Soviet Union was cemented by joint membership in two international organizations. One—the Council for Mutual Economic Assistance, or COMECON—was economic. It was established in 1948 to formulate joint economic policies for all members of the Soviet bloc. The other—the Communist Information Bureau, or COMINFORM—was ideological. In addition to the Communist parties of the Soviet bloc, it included the Italian and French Communist parties.

The COMINFORM was the main Communist propaganda mill, churning out what anti-Communists called the "party line" that all Soviet-style Communists were expected to parrot. Through it, the Soviet Communist party essentially told the other European parties what policies to follow. Little dissent was tolerated.

THE COLD WAR

The increasing unity of the Soviet bloc frightened the Western nations. Ideologically, the Communists were sworn enemies of capitalism. They talked of world revolution and of workers overthrowing capitalist governments everywhere. Militarily, the nations of western Europe felt particularly threatened because they faced the prospect of a united, Soviet-dominated Eastern Europe. The United States, which had just taken part in two world wars that had begun in Eastern Europe, shared their fears.

Those fears increased in April 1948, when the Soviets blockaded Berlin. They denied access to Western trains, trucks, and boats that were bringing goods into the divided city through Soviet-occupied eastern Germany. They hoped the blockade would force the Allies to give up their zones of the city. But the Allies managed to break the blockade with an enormous airlift, and the Soviets eventually accepted the Western presence in Berlin.

The following year, the Allies sponsored the birth of the Federal Republic of Germany, a new, Western-style democracy established in the Allied-occupied zones of Germany. In response, the Soviet Union supported the formation of a new nation in the Soviet-occupied territory, which was called the German Democratic Republic (GDR). The new entities quickly became better known simply as West Germany and East Germany.

These events convinced the Allies once and for all that they needed to do something to counter Soviet power in Europe. On April 4, 1949, representatives of the Western nations signed the historic North Atlantic Treaty. In it, they established a new military alliance, agreeing to consider an attack on any one of them an attack on all of them. They also set up a new international body, known as NATO (North Atlantic Treaty Organization), through which they would help each other to promote their mutual security. The charter members of NATO were the United States, Belgium, Canada, Denmark, France, Great Britain, Iceland, Italy, Luxembourg, the Netherlands, Norway, and Portugal. Greece, Turkey, West Germany, and Spain joined later. One of the long-term results of this treaty was the stationing of a more or less permanent U.S. military force in Europe. It is still there.

It was obvious to everyone that NATO had been designed to confront a single enemy: the Soviet Union. Faced with such a powerful military alliance forming ranks against it, the USSR formed a military alliance of its own on March 14, 1955. Known as the Warsaw Treaty Organization and commonly referred to as the Warsaw Pact, it consisted of the Soviet Union, Bulgaria, Czechoslovakia, Hungary, Poland, Romania, and Albania.

(Albania is a small country on the western rim of the Balkan Peninsula. Like Yugoslavia, it became Communist after the war but was never really a Soviet satellite. It preferred the Chinese style of communism to that of the Soviet Union. The USSR broke off diplomatic relations with Albania in 1961. Seven years later, Albania pulled out of the Warsaw Pact. It eventually broke with China as well.)

The formation of NATO and the Warsaw Pact was a major escalation (stepping up) of what the physicist P. M. S. Blackett once called the "cold diplomatic war with Russia."[11] The two alliances effectively enlisted most of Europe on one side or the other in what became known as the "cold war" between the superpowers.

There followed a long period of fear, bluff, and escalation: preparation for a possible "hot" war that might break out at any time. It seemed to many on both sides that the Communist and capitalist nations were on a collision course. As the American president Dwight Eisenhower expressed it, "We face a hostile ideology—global in scope, atheistic in character, ruthless in purpose, and insidious in method. Unhappily, the danger it poses promises to be of infinite duration."[12] At the same time, the Soviets felt themselves in constant danger from the hostile, capitalist West. Many people on both sides became convinced that sometime, somehow, there would have to be a final battle between them to settle the matter.

The terrible power of the atom bomb—and later, of other nuclear weapons—added a special horror to the threat of conflict between the West and the East. The United States had already used atomic weapons against Japan. Once the Soviet Union developed its own bomb in 1949, the cold war became a balance of terror. Three years later, the United States attempted to upset the balance in its favor when it developed the even more powerful hydrogen bomb. But within a year after that, the Soviets developed that weapon too. And so it went. Before long, each side had developed the power to destroy all human and animal life on the planet many times over. For more than thirty years, the people of the world had to live in constant fear that the two superpowers might do just that at any moment.

In their backyards, people dug "fallout shelters" they hoped would protect them from nuclear attack. American children who went to school in the 1950s and early 1960s carried out regular drills, like fire drills, in which they practiced diving under their desks to protect themselves from fallout when the dreaded bombs finally fell.

Both sides devoted immense amounts of resources to preparing for the nuclear war that might be

74

coming. In the meantime, they fought (or supported others who fought) "small" wars in places like Korea, Vietnam, and Afghanistan. How much all of this cost the two sides is impossible to say, because many of the expenses were hidden. But by 1960, at least 50 percent of the U.S. budget was going to military expenditures, and military spending went up dramatically throughout the rest of the 1960s. Probably even higher percentages of Soviet resources went into the cold war. Although the proportion of the U.S. budget devoted to military spending has dropped in recent decades, the actual amounts spent on both sides' military forces have continued to soar.

6
"THE BREATH OF TRUTH"

From the outside, the nations of the Warsaw Pact seemed to march along in happy lockstep with the Soviet Union. Their governments, dominated by powerful national Communist party organizations, were apparently content to follow the Soviets' lead blindly. The ordinary citizens, meanwhile, had little to say about it. Many of them assumed that they could do nothing to influence events. Others agreed with their governments that communism was the best answer to their problems and that neither national independence nor individual political rights were particularly important.

But all was never as peaceful as it seemed inside the Soviet bloc. The people were not nearly as brainwashed as they appeared to be. Even some of their leaders were not as happy to follow the Soviet model as they seemed. Over and over again during the 1950s and 1960s, underlying churnings of discontent would bubble to the surface and break out into public view.

"DE-STALINIZATION"

Even within the Soviet Union itself, political peace could be kept only by massive government repression. Under Stalin, all political opposition that arose was brutally crushed. Even longtime Communist leaders who spoke out against Stalin's regime were swiftly exiled to Siberia—if they were not simply taken out and shot. One way or another, millions of lives were disrupted or destroyed by Stalin's oppression.

After Joseph Stalin's death in 1953, a new generation of Communist leaders, led by Premier Nikita Khrushchev, took over in the Soviet Union. They began a process of "de-Stalinization"—reforms that loosened some of the chains that bound the people of the Soviet Union. Khrushchev himself gave a "Secret Report" to the 20th Communist Party Congress, condemning Stalin's regime for its many crimes.[1]

De-Stalinization also loosened the chains that bound the Soviet Union and its satellites. In the past, the COMINFORM had always laid down what amounted to strict guidelines the satellites had to follow. Now the satellites were given more autonomy, more freedom to choose their own domestic policies. Khrushchev even spoke of there being "several roads to socialism." The COMINFORM was abolished in 1956.

These reforms only loosened the chains that bound the nations of the Soviet bloc, however; they did not remove them. The countries of Eastern Europe were freer now to experiment and to set policies for themselves, but they were not free to go their own way. The difference was not clear. The new limits had to be tested.

THE POLISH OCTOBER OF 1956

The Poles were the first to take advantage of the loosening of their chains. In June 1956, workers' strikes there were followed by demonstrations against Soviet control. Although the authorities soon put an end to the strikes, the unrest continued. That October, the Communist government of Poland moved to adjust itself to the mood of the people. It threw out its old-line Stalinist leaders and replaced them with a new and more liberal, or broad-minded, Communist leadership. At its head was Wladislaw Gomulka, a Communist reformer newly released from prison, where he had been held for years because of his opposition to the old regime.

The new regime acted quickly to launch a series of reforms that became known as the "Polish October." Almost all of the relatively few Polish farms that had been collectivized were returned to private hands.[2] Almost overnight, open political debate became possible in Poland, something that had never happened before in *any* Soviet bloc country. And most astonishing of all, the Soviets put up with these reforms! Although the Soviet bear growled a little, and Khrushchev himself visited Poland, no real action was taken to put down the new liberalism in Poland.

THE HUNGARIAN REVOLT

Similar events were taking place in Hungary. Students, workers, and intellectual dissidents (opponents of the government) staged large anti-government demonstrations there that same October. When the government moved in to put an end to the demonstrations, the demonstrators rebelled. The Hungarian army was ordered to crush the rebellion, but the troops took the protesters' side instead. With the country facing a growing revolt, a liberal and nationalist Communist named Imre Nagy was made head of the government.

The Soviet government worried that the dissatisfaction with the governments it supported in its satellites could produce a growing hostility toward the Warsaw Pact. Attempting to calm the unrest, it granted concessions. It announced that in the future it would treat the other members of the Warsaw Pact more respectfully. It would even withdraw its troops from their countries if that was what the local governments wanted.

But Imre Nagy's government was not satisfied with such concessions—it didn't want its chains loosened; it wanted them broken—and announced its intention to withdraw from the Warsaw Pact altogether. What is more, Nagy declared, in the future Hungary would be neutral in the cold war. He even asked the United Nations to protect Hungary from foreign—that is, Soviet—interference.

This was a clear challenge, not just to the Warsaw Pact but to the Soviet Union, which reacted by sending troops into the Hungarian capital city of Budapest. They seized the city and installed a new pro-Soviet government under Janos Kadar (meanwhile, Soviet security forces kidnapped Premier Nagy near the Yugoslav embassy[3]). The Hungarians fought back as well as they could, but within a few weeks the much stronger Soviet forces had crushed their spirited rebellion.

But even after the armed resistance ended, the Hungarians continued to protest Soviet domination. Many workers went on strike, and others refused to cooperate with the new government.

Through it all, the rebels had hoped for support from the United Nations or from Western countries like the United States. After all, many voices around the world had been raised in support of Hungary's rebellion. Many Western countries had welcomed the action, and even the Communist party newspaper in Poland denounced the Soviets for using "Stalinist" methods in Hungary.[4] But all of the cheering came from the sidelines. No one came to help the Hungarians when the Soviets attacked.

The Kadar government later announced that 20,000 Hungarians had been either killed or injured in the rebellion. The real number of casualties was probably much higher. Nor were they the last to suffer from the crushing of the Hungarian revolt. Another 2,000 people were executed, at least 20,000 more were sent to prison, and an uncounted number of others were sent to labor camps inside the Soviet Union.[5]

THE PRAGUE SPRING OF 1968

In 1968, there was another great outbreak of freedom in the Soviet bloc. That was a year of political upheaval in many countries all around the world. In France, left-wing students were taking to the streets in a daring effort to bring down the government of President Charles de Gaulle. In the United States, there were massive demonstrations against the war in Vietnam, poverty, and racial injustice. And in Czechoslovakia, the government joined with the people in the streets to launch a bold thrust toward freedom and independence.

Led by a moderate Communist party leader named Alexander Dubček, the Czechoslovakian government began a dramatic process of radical reform in the spring of 1968. Dubček spoke of establishing "socialism with a human face" in Czechoslovakia—a truly democratic form of communism that would not impose itself through force and terror.

This period of liberalization came to be known as the "Prague Spring." It included an attempt to decentralize the Czechoslovak economy, as well as to grant the freedoms of speech, assembly, press, and religion to the people of Czechoslovakia. Domestically, the ethnic tensions between the Czechs and the Slovaks were to be eased by granting Slovakia a special semiautonomous status within the country. In foreign policy, there was to be a loosening of the ties to the Soviet Union and an increase of trade with the West.

Students publicly debated the pros and cons of capitalism, socialism, and communism. Western-style folksingers strummed guitars and sang songs of love and protest in the streets. There was a sudden flowering of the arts, unlike anything that had been seen in Eastern Europe since the falling of the iron curtain twenty years before. For a few brief weeks, there was a sense of celebration—almost of joy—as Czechoslovakians experienced the thrilling new sense of freedom.

But the Prague Spring frightened the Soviet leaders more than anything had since 1956. Leaders in some of the other satellites were welcoming the Czechoslovakian experiment. If it succeeded, the infection of reform might spread. In May, Dubček was flown to Moscow and warned that he was going too far. Soviet troops were brought to the Czechslovakian border. But the reforms continued. In July, a number of Warsaw Pact governments sent a joint letter to Dubček saying that the situation in his country was "absolutely unacceptable."[6] In May, almost the entire Soviet leadership went to Czechoslovakia to persuade the Czech government to end its reforms.

Other Eastern European leaders (including Kadar of Hungary and Nicolae Ceauşescu of Romania) tried to persuade the Czechs to escape a showdown with the Soviet Union by abandoning at least some of the reforms. Even President Tito of Yugoslavia tried to get Dubček to back down. Under the pressure, a reluctant Dubček agreed to keep Czechoslovakia in the Warsaw Pact and to preserve the special role of the Communist party within Czechoslovakia.

But this late attempt at compromise was not enough. On August 20, Soviet troops invaded Czechoslovakia. They were joined in the attack by Warsaw Pact troops from East Germany, Poland, Hungary, and Bulgaria. Only Romania refused to join in crushing Czechoslovakia's brave experiment.

The Warsaw Pact invasion was sudden, massive, and totally successful. Hundreds of thousands of Warsaw Pact soldiers streamed across the border in trucks and tanks. The skies above Prague were filled with planes carrying troops and supplies to the Czechoslovakian capital. There was little armed resistance. The Czechoslovakians knew they had no chance to win a battle against the huge forces massed against them.

With the liberal experiment dismantled, the Soviets kept Dubček in office until April 1969. At that time, however, the government was turned over to a more hard-line Communist named Gustav Husak. Under Husak, Czechoslovakia became one of the most strictly controlled of all of the satellite countries, with the most centralized economy in all of Europe. Even the Soviet Union would allow a higher proportion of goods to be produced by private means than Czechoslovakia would. Czechoslovakia's ambassador to the United States Rita Klimova has said, "Everything belonged to the state."[7]

THE BREZHNEV DOCTRINE

The hopefulness of the Prague Spring and the violence of the summer of 1968 were followed by a long, cold winter throughout the Soviet bloc. The Czecho-slovakian crisis resulted in a policy that became known as the Brezhnev Doctrine. Soviet premier Leonid Brezhnev announced a doctrine of "limited sovereignty," restricting the right of any Warsaw Pact country to stray too far away from what the others, particularly the Soviets, considered acceptable Communist principles.

The essence of the doctrine was spelled out in a letter from five members of the Warsaw Pact to the Dubček government in July 1968: "Our [national Communist] parties must answer for their actions not only to their own working-class, but also to the international working-class and to the international Communist movement," the letter said.[8] In other words, the Communist states of Europe had the right to intervene in each other's affairs. It was that "right" that the same five countries would claim gave them the authority to invade Czechoslovakia only a month later.

The Brezhnev Doctrine was in direct opposition to the policies established by Lenin after the Soviet revolution. But the Soviet Union had seen Yugoslavia get away, and it watched nervously as Romania, Poland, Hungary, and Czechoslovakia all asserted a greater amount of independence. It was, in Brezhnev's view, time to draw the line. Any future moves toward independence would have to be approved, or they would be crushed.

Thanks to the Brezhnev Doctrine, the Czechoslovakian experiment was the last of its kind for twenty years. During most of that time, it seemed that the people of Eastern Europe had accepted their nations' status as satellite states of the Soviet Union—or at least had given up all hope of doing anything about it.

And yet, somehow, the instincts that had found expression in Poland and Hungary in 1956 and in

Czechoslovakia in 1968 remained alive. Resentment of the Soviet Union, a longing for independence, and a disgust with their own countries' puppet governments were still churning beneath the surface, waiting to break free.

That freedom would finally come in 1989. When it did, some would remember what had happened two decades before. At that time, the dissident Soviet scientist Andrei Sakharov would write to Alexander Dubček, "I am convinced that the breath of truth that the Czechs and the Slovaks inhaled [in 1968] . . . is the prologue to today's bloodless revolutions in the countries of Eastern Europe."[9]

7
THE FOUNDATIONS FOR CHANGE

The foundations for the dramatic changes of 1989 had been laid earlier in the decade, in two countries—Poland and the Soviet Union.

SOLIDARITY

As a group, the Polish people had always been strongly nationalistic and Roman Catholic. Both elements in their character were strengthened in 1978, when a firmly anti-Communist Polish cardinal, Karol Wojtyla, was elected pope—the leader of the Catholic church throughout the world. Wojtyla, who took the name John Paul II, was not only the first Polish pope in history, he was the first pope since 1523 to come from anywhere but Italy.

In Poland, his election was considered a "miracle." People rushed into the streets to celebrate. Even the officially atheist Communist government had to announce its pleasure that a Pole had been chosen head of the Roman Catholic church.[1]

In 1979, the new pope made a trip through Poland. It set off an outpouring of affection and national pride like nothing seen in the country in the twentieth century. Looking back, some observers now believe that it was the election of Pope John Paul II, as much as anything else, that gave the Poles the sense of pride and confidence that would carry them through to independence ten years later.

But before they could achieve that independence, they needed a movement through which to organize. That movement, it turned out, was born the year after the pope's visit. In July 1980, the Polish government (which, like many of the other Eastern European governments, controlled most prices) doubled the price of meat. Similar rises had set off strikes and riots in 1970 and again in 1976. The alarmed government had called out the troops to crush them. More than 45 people had been killed in the violence in 1970, and over 1,000 had been injured.

Now there was a new series of strikes. If the price of food was going to soar, the workers reasoned, they would need more money to pay for it. Many factories quickly granted small wage increases to keep the peace, but it wasn't enough to satisfy the workers.

The government responded to the strikes of 1980 by throwing several of the leaders and dissidents into jail, mostly for short periods of time. But nothing stopped the strikes from spreading.

The key events of 1980 began in August in the city of Gdansk. In that month, a small number of the 16,000 workers at the Lenin Shipyards there decided to go on strike. Meeting in a large open space inside the shipyards, they called on their fellow workers to join them. But the manager of the factory promised negotiations, and the strike seemed about to fail. Just then, a dissident climbed over the fence from outside the factory and addressed the crowd. His name was

Lech Walesa. He had once worked at the shipyards, and his opinions still carried weight with many of the workers there. When he joined in the strikers' appeal, most of them decided to go ahead with it. On August 23, the great majority, if not all, of the 16,000 went out on strike. But instead of leaving, they decided to occupy the premises, preventing new workers from being brought in and effectively shutting the shipyards down.[2]

Among the workers' demands was the right to form an independent union. (There were "unions" in Poland, but they were effectively controlled by the Communist government, not by the workers.) It would be based on a strike committee, formed in Gdansk, that soon was representing workers in hundreds of factories.

As a tool in communicating with its members, the committee began issuing mimeographed bulletins. It called its little publication *Solidarnosc,* the Polish word for "solidarity," a term traditionally used by workers (and by Communists) around the world.

The strike was settled within two weeks. The government made a number of important concessions, including better working conditions, a relaxation of censorship in Poland, and recognition of an independent union. Walesa was established as head of the union, which took the name Solidarity. Within a short time, it was claiming 8 million members throughout Poland. Out in the Polish countryside, the farmers organized a union of their own, which they called Rural Solidarity.

It wasn't long before the agreement fell apart. The government refused to keep many of its promises and put off official recognition of Rural Solidarity. A Polish court even refused to recognize Solidarity itself unless the union acknowledged the authority of the Communist party, which the union refused to do.

Eventually, both of the unions were officially recognized, but in the meantime the economic and political crisis in Poland kept growing worse. Solidarity became the rallying point for all of the antigovernment feeling in the country.

The tensions inside Poland alarmed its Communist neighbors. The Soviet Union, East Germany, and Czechoslovakia all began to put pressure on the Polish government. If a strong independent union were established in Poland, demands for independent unions could spread to the other nations of the Warsaw Pact. What was worse, a truly independent union could be a serious rival to the Communist party and therefore a serious threat to any Communist government.

By the spring of 1981, the fear began to spread that the Warsaw Pact countries might invade Poland, as they had invaded Czechoslovakia in 1968. Just as the Pact's leaders had done then, they were issuing warnings that things were going too far. Ironically, one of the strongest warnings of all came from Gustav Husak of Czechoslovakia.

Meanwhile, serious splits were becoming obvious within Solidarity. At a union congress held in September 1981, some of delegates challenged Walesa's leadership, charging that he was not paying enough attention to the demands of the ordinary workers. Although Walesa (who was proving to be a master politician) managed to hold on to his position as head of the union, several of the protesters were elected to other offices.

The economic situation in Poland got even worse in October, when the government announced another round of stiff increases in the price of food. A three-way negotiation was held between General Wojciech Jaruzelski, who headed the Polish government; Walesa, representing Solidarity; and Archbishop Jozef Glemp, representing the Polish Catholic church. They tried to find some way out of the deepening crisis but failed. There was a brief reduction in prices, as a concession to Solidarity, but they soon rose again. By the middle of the month, strikes were again breaking out around the country, this time without approval from Solidarity. Even appeals from the union, asking workers to reduce the growing tensions by going back to work, were often ignored. There were outbreaks of violence between protesters and police.

Things came to a head in December. At a meeting of the national Solidarity leadership in Gdansk, Walesa appealed for moderation. "I declare with my full authority," he proclaimed, "we are for agreement. . . . We do *not* want any confrontation."[3] But Walesa's appeal was not enough. Other, more radical leaders seemed determined to invite a showdown with the government. Ignoring his protests, they passed measures calling for a one-day general strike across Poland, followed by a nationwide poll that would directly challenge the Communist party's role in the government. They had gone too far. Even if Jaruzelski had been willing to put up with the challenge to his party's authority, it's unlikely the Soviet Union would have.

As it turned out, Jaruzelski was *not* willing to put up with it. Perhaps he had been waiting for an excuse to crush Solidarity all along. Or perhaps he was afraid that if he didn't act soon, the other Warsaw Pact nations would invade Poland. In any case, his response was sudden and sweeping.

On the night of Saturday, December 12, Polish troops took charge of every major city in Poland. All communications were cut off. The Solidarity leaders in Gdansk were taken into custody. Walesa was separated from the others and taken out of the city. He would be confined to "house arrest" in a distant hunting lodge for eleven months.[4]

At six o'clock that Sunday morning, while the people of Poland were waking up, unaware of what had happened overnight, General Jaruzelski formally announced that a state of war existed in Poland. He declared martial law, temporarily ending all civil rights in the country.[5]

Even so, Solidarity managed to organize some large demonstrations in the spring of 1982 and to keep operating through the summer. But in October, the Sejm (the Polish parliament) officially dissolved Solidarity. Before Christmas, the government felt strong enough to suspend martial law and to allow Walesa to return to Gdansk.

The government had won the first round of battles between itself and Solidarity. But seven years later, Solidarity would win the war.

GORBACHEV COMES TO POWER IN THE SOVIET UNION

When liberalization finally came to Eastern Europe, it came first to the most unlikely place of all—the Soviet Union. In a sense, the momentous forces that would transform Eastern Europe in 1989 began to work in the Soviet Union in 1985. That was the year that a new leader, Mikhail S. Gorbachev, was named chairman of the Communist party of the Soviet Union.

Gorbachev inherited a one-party Communist system that was politically paralyzed and economically bankrupt. The Communist party had held a political and economic monopoly for more than seventy years, but it had failed to win the full support of its people or to build a strong economy.

Politically, it had concentrated more on holding on to its own power than on solving the huge nation's many problems. In the process, it had alienated great masses of the people. It had lost their trust, and worse, it had lost their confidence in its ability to function.

Some of the government's biggest failures had been in the area of economics: the basic bread-and-butter issues of providing food, clothing, and shelter for its people. Despite the government's monopoly on the means of production—or perhaps because of it—the Soviet economy was notoriously inefficient. Even with the enormous resources of a vast and varied country, it could not produce nearly enough goods to satisfy the needs of the people.

One reason was that for decades an enormous amount of those resources had gone to the military. The arms race with the West was a terrible drain on the nation's economy. Raw materials and labor that went into weapons were not available for producing goods and services. The result was a huge and apparently powerful military machine but very little else.

Housing was so scarce in many cities that people had to wait years to qualify for an apartment. It was said that, in some towns, people had to wait thirteen years just to get a telephone. There were frequent shortages of certain kinds of food and constant shortages of others. Even the most ordinary consumer goods, from clothing to radios, were often hard to find and usually poorly made. Soviet cars, for example, were considered among the worst in the world. Many modern consumer goods that people in the West took for granted—from soft drinks to videotape machines—couldn't be found at all.

By the time Gorbachev took power, even the effectiveness of the Soviet Union's enormous military machine was in question. Its nuclear arsenal was huge but necessarily untested. When a meltdown at a civilian nuclear power plant near Chernobyl sent clouds of radiation rolling over Europe in 1986, people began to wonder whether any Soviet nuclear facilities, civilian or military, could really be relied on.

Meanwhile, the Soviet Union's huge conventional army was bogged down in Afghanistan. It had been in a war there for six years, fighting a rebel guerrilla force that it could not defeat. For all its supposed might, the Soviet army—bigger than any other in Europe, bigger even than that of the United States—was unable to win even a small war, in a half-primitive country, on its own border. It was a lesson that the United States had already learned about its own military in Vietnam, but that didn't ease the Soviets' sense of frustration.

Gorbachev was unusual among recent Soviet rulers in that he admitted that the situation in the Soviet Union was bad and that something drastic had to be done about it. In fact, many things had to be done. In a flurry of reforms, he set about trying to do at least some of them. Those reforms came to be known by the Russian words *perestroika* (which means "restructuring") and *glasnost* (which means "openness").

PERESTROIKA

Gorbachev tried to improve production by giving more authority to factory managers and less to minor government officials who had gotten used to telling factories how to operate. He pushed through legislation that allowed more small private businesses and cooperatives to be formed. In addition, he made clear that he was hoping to introduce at least some elements of competition and free market pricing into the Soviet economy in the future.

Perestroika was extremely controversial, both inside the Soviet Union and outside in the West. Gorbachev, who claimed to be a good Communist, insisted that *perestroika* did not mean abandoning communism. Instead, it was an attempt to rescue the system from its past mistakes. *Perestroika* was designed to make communism work as an economic system by mixing it with some capitalist-like reforms. "Our ideal," Gorbachev proclaimed, "is a humane, democratic socialism."[6] Nonetheless, the conservative, old-style Communists within the Soviet Union were appalled by the reforms. They considered them betrayals of the Marxism many of them had genuinely believed in.

At the same time, those who welcomed the reforms complained that they did not go nearly far enough. It was like giving a desperately ill patient medicine that was badly watered down. The Soviet economy, the critics claimed, was far too sick to be healed by the timid measures Gorbachev prescribed.[7]

GLASNOST

The changes that were carried out under the new policy of *glasnost* were much more sweeping and dramatic. Before Gorbachev, Soviet society had been one of the most closed and restrictive in history. Now, practically without warning, it was thrown open to a degree not seen since before the revolution of 1917, if ever.

In the past, the government could do no wrong. Khrushchev's attack on Stalinism had shocked the world in 1956 because the Soviets never allowed public criticism of their system. Following that, the system closed down again. The few voices raised in criticism inside the Soviet Union were quickly silenced. Dissidents like the scientist Andrei Sakharov and the writer Alexander Solzhenitsyn had been exiled or jailed. Some had been tortured and virtually starved to death in prison.

Suddenly, Soviet government officials began actually *admitting* past mistakes. Even more astonishing, they allowed ordinary citizens to criticize the government as well. Many dissidents, including Sakharov, were released from prison. Non-Communist political groups were allowed to function and even to run candidates for political office. The first multiparty elections were held in 1987.

In the past, the jobs of Soviet officials and bureaucrats had been safe. The only way they could lose their jobs and power was by offending someone higher up in the party. But now thousands of minor officials were actually thrown out of office for abusing their power and for violating other citizens' civil rights.

One of the most startling of all of the changes was the lessening of the stifling secrecy that had always been central to the Soviet way of life. Suddenly political ideas could be openly debated. Events could be publicly reported that could never even have been mentioned before. For decades, the government had managed the news in a determined effort to pretend that everything was going well in the Soviet Union. Even news of major accidents had been hidden from the Soviet public. But now such things were widely reported in the government-controlled press. When the disastrous meltdown took place at Chernobyl, people were almost as astonished to find it discussed in the Soviet press as they were appalled by the tragic accident itself.

In the past, Communist party congresses had been held in great secrecy. Only party members in good standing were allowed inside. What was said there, and by whom, was guarded as a state secret. But in 1990, when the historic 28th Party Congress was held in Moscow, it was carried on television—and not just in the Soviet Union. It was made available, live and unedited, to viewers around the world.[8]

Gorbachev even carried *glasnost* to the United States when he visited in 1990. Conducting a frank meeting with U.S. Congressional leaders, he allowed American news organizations to televise it. (Ironically, although the Soviet leader was perfectly willing to air his opinions before the world, some of the American politicians were extremely annoyed when they learned that their remarks were being made public.)

But reforms inside the Soviet Union were one thing; reforms in the Soviet Union's satellites were another. Would Gorbachev be as liberal with the nations of the Soviet bloc as he was with his own people?

It was not long before it became clear that the answer was yes. Although there would be moments of real tension between the Soviet Union and its satellites during the tumultuous events of 1989, in the end Gorbachev was willing to let them go. In fact, at times, he almost seemed to be encouraging them to leave.

8
THE PEACEFUL
REVOLUTIONS OF 1989

In 1989, the political and diplomatic realities that Europe had lived with for more than forty years changed overnight. Everything changed. Regimes that had been among the strongest and most unyielding in modern history collapsed without warning. Mortal enemies became friends. Politicians who had competed with each other in their devotion to old-style communism suddenly began competing to show their devotion to reform. And—most remarkable of all—the Soviet Union loosened its grip on Eastern Europe without a fight. The dreaded iron curtain came drifting down, as easily and as gently as if it were made of lace.

SOLIDARITY TRIUMPHS IN POLAND

Although the Solidarity union had been outlawed in 1982, its spirit hadn't died. That living spirit was saluted the year after the banning, when Lech Walesa was awarded the 1983 Nobel Prize for Peace.

Perhaps the most symbolic image of the fall of communism
in Eastern Europe is the dismantling of the Berlin Wall, which
for almost thirty years served as a grim reminder of a world divided.

As the government of Czechoslovakia lost its power to intimidate the people, hundreds of thousands of demonstrators took to the streets to stage what came to be known as the "Velvet Revolution."

Ivan III, grand duke of Muscovy from 1462 to 1505, was the first ruler to solidify the Russian state and expand westward.

Peter the Great knew that the only way to strengthen his country was through the introduction of Western technology and culture. In addition, as a result of his bold military exploits, Russia was finally acknowledged as a formidable power in Europe.

Catherine the Great, in a conspiracy with King Frederick II of Prussia, took several large portions of Poland, marking the beginning of Russian territorial expansion into eastern Europe.

With the end of the Napoleonic Wars, the czar of Russia was also named king of Poland. Nicholas I proved to be ruthless in his new role as "policeman of Europe," brutally crushing a rebellion in 1830.

Due to desperate poverty, many peasants and industrial workers turned to bolshevism during the nineteenth century.

Joseph Stalin (left) shakes hands with German Foreign Minister
Joachim von Ribbentrop, upon signing of the Nazi-Soviet
Nonaggression Pact, in August 1939. Russia once again laid
claims to lands in eastern Poland, which since World War I had
been enjoying national independence.

Above: In February 1945, the "Big Three"—Churchill, Roosevelt, and Stalin—met in Yalta to discuss the shaping of the postwar era. Although Stalin, right, requested only a strip of eastern Poland at this conference, he actually intended to extend Soviet influence to Eastern Europe. Below: Winston Churchill, before the "Iron Curtain" speech. It is generally believed that the cold war began with this speech, in which he warned of the dangers of communism and called for unity among the Western nations.

A U.S. plane drops down candy to children in West Berlin during the Soviet blockade of 1948.

After Stalin's death in 1953, Soviet premier Nikita Khrushchev eased
restrictions governing domestic policies in Eastern European nations.

Above: Hungarian rebels ride through the streets of Budapest in a captured Soviet tank in 1956. Although Khrushchev was willing to grant certain reforms, he would not tolerate Hungary's withdrawal from the Warsaw Pact, and the rebellion was quickly put down. Below: In 1968, Czechoslovakia's demands for greater autonomy were met with thousands of heavily armed Warsaw Pact troops.

Under the direction of Lech Walesa, Polish workers formed
Solidarity, an independent labor union that successfully challenged
the Communist regime.

Through Soviet premier Mikhail Gorbachev's policies of economic and social reform, the movement toward independence in Eastern Europe became a reality.

Vaclav Havel, a popular playwright imprisoned several times for what was deemed subversive writing, was named president of Czechoslovakia shortly after the "Velvet Revolution," and was formally elected in June 1990.

Not all of the revolutions of 1989 were as peaceful as those that took place in Poland, Hungary, and Czechoslovakia. In Romania antigovernment protests and a civil war between the army and the national security police left hundreds dead.

One of the greatest problems facing the newly liberated countries of Eastern Europe is cleaning up the environment. In Copsa Mica, Romania (above), as well as in the Silesia region of Poland (below), several dangerous pollutants have been carelessly dumped into local soils and waterways.

With the end of communism in Eastern Europe, other nations have
begun to assert their demands for freedom. Here demonstrators
in Vilnius, the capital of Lithuania, stage an independence rally
that drew 300,000 people.

The Nobel Peace Prize may be the most prestigious award in the world. Previous winners had included Dr. Martin Luther King, Jr., of the United States and Mother Teresa of India. But the award was not meant just for Walesa. It was meant for the organization he had helped to found. In the eyes of the world, it put Solidarity on a level with the other great organizations that had received the prize in the past, including the United Nations Children's Fund (UNICEF) and the International Red Cross.

The spirit of Solidarity was kept alive for the next seven years by activist workers, students, artists, and intellectuals. Acting in the open when possible, and underground when necessary, they built what they called a "parallel culture" to the one established by the Communist government. They ran underground health clinics and universities; they wrote, printed, and distributed thousands of pamphlets, books, and newspapers attacking the government and calling for freedom in Poland.[1]

And all the while, Poland was slipping deeper and deeper into an economic mudhole. With $40 billion in foreign debt eating up the few goods it could produce, the economy was scarcely able to keep the Poles fed and clothed. The people were becoming more and more desperate as food prices continued to rise, wages stayed stubbornly low, and even the necessities of life became harder and harder to scrape together.

The more desperate the people got, the angrier they became. Most of that anger was directed at the government. After all, it was the government that set both prices and wages. If the prices were too high for them to pay out of the wages they received, it must be the government's fault. The only way most workers had to protest the worsening situation was to go on strike. In Communist Poland, that meant striking against the government, which owned most of the major industries.

By 1988, a growing number of strikes was crippling what was left of the Polish economy. Jaruzelski and his government were getting almost as desperate as the people. Something had to be done. Some way had to be found to bring industrial peace to the country. Short of a massive and brutal military crackdown, the only way out of the crisis was negotiation.

But whom could the government negotiate with? How does a despised dictatorial government negotiate with its own people? There was no officially recognized political opposition in the country. The Communist party had never allowed an effective legal opposition party to form. If a deal was to be made, it would have to be made with Solidarity—a union that did not even legally exist.

Reluctantly, the government agreed to negotiate with Solidarity. On April 5, 1989, the deal was struck, and a truly revolutionary agreement was signed between the Communist government and the illegal union. According to its provisions, three banned organizations—Solidarity, Rural Solidarity, and the Independent Student Association—would all be made legal. The income of Polish workers and the elderly would be tied to rises in the cost of living; when prices went up, incomes would go up as well. And most historic of all, free elections would be held in Poland the following June.[2]

The June elections were for seats in the Sejm, as well as in a completely new house of parliament, the Senate. Under the ground rules that had been agreed to in April, Solidarity's candidates would be able to run for all of the seats in the Senate, although 65 percent of the seats in the Sejm would be reserved for candidates from the so-called Communist bloc (that is, members either of the Communist party or of two smaller parties that were allied with the Communists).

When the election results were in, Solidarity candidates had won 260 of the 261 seats they'd been allowed to run for. In most cases, they'd defeated their Communist opponents by a large margin. The Communist defeat was even more devastating than the Solidarity victory was impressive. Not only had many Communist-bloc candidates lost to opposition candidates but thirty-three of the thirty-five Communist-bloc candidates who'd run totally unopposed failed to get the 50 percent of the votes they needed to be officially elected![3]

In a compromise worked out between Solidarity and the Communists, General Jaruzelski was elected the first president. But Solidarity balked when Jaruzelski suggested a fellow Communist, General Czeslaw Kiszczak, for the powerful post of prime minister. (Under the Polish system, the president could nominate a candidate, but the choice had to be approved by the Sejm.) Neither Solidarity nor the Communists held a majority in the Sejm. The balance of power was held by the two minor parties of the Communist bloc. But reading the overwhelming results of the election, they abandoned the Communist party to join forces with Solidarity. As a result, a Solidarity member, Tadeusz Mazowiecki, was chosen prime minister on August 24, 1989.[4]

Mazowiecki had the responsibility of forming a government, that is, of picking the twenty-four cabinet officials who would help set government policies and administer government programs. Only four of the twenty-four ministries were given to Communists. The Communist party considered refusing to join in the new government, until Mikhail Gorbachev himself called to urge Poland's Communist party to cooperate with Solidarity.[5]

Despite the Communist presence in the government, it was clear to everyone that Solidarity, not the Communist party, was now in control. It was the first non-Communist-led government ever allowed in the Soviet bloc.

When a boulder is dislodged at the top of a mountain, it begins to roll downhill. As it picks up speed, it sets off a chain reaction, bumping into other boulders that in turn bump into more and more others. Pretty soon, the whole mountainside is in motion.

Something like that happened in Eastern Europe in 1989. The fall of the Communist government in Poland was the first boulder. It set off a political avalanche as, one after another, the governments of Eastern Europe began to roll. Before the year was out, the entire mountainside was in motion.

HUNGARY OPENS A GATEWAY TO THE WEST

Long before 1989, Hungary had been the most progressive country in Eastern Europe. Although the Communist party was in control of the government and of most major elements of the economy, Hungary had been experimenting with capitalist economic measures since 1968.[6] In that year, the government introduced its "New Economic Mechanism," a series of policies that bore a suspicious resemblance to certain elements of capitalist economies. The new policies called for more decentralization than most Communist countries allowed, as well as a greater reliance on the market forces of supply and demand. It even provided for a reinstatement of the profit motive.[7]

Although the government continued to own and operate many of the big industries, small private businesses were also allowed—and even encouraged.

100

Tourism from Western countries and investment by Western businesses were both actively courted.

Perhaps the most surprising indication of Hungary's flirtation with the West was the Formula 1 auto race held there each year. Formula 1 is a showcase of Western wealth and technology. It is the glamorous testing ground for the most highly developed—and expensive—cars in the world. The cheapest cars on a Formula 1 track cost over $1 million apiece. The top drivers receive several million dollars each year. It would be impossible to imagine any country in the Soviet bloc allowing such a flaunting of capitalist wealth, much less welcoming it. But Hungary did.

Politically, too, Hungary was surprisingly progressive for an Eastern European country. It allowed its people a fairly high degree of freedom of expression; and although it was a one-party state, the Hungarian Communist party was more open to ideas and influences from other elements of society than were the other Communist parties in Eastern Europe.

It is not surprising, then, that Hungary was one of the first countries to start liberalizing in 1989. The Hungarian Parliament formally approved freedom of association and assembly in January. The following month, the ruling party okayed the formation of independent, non-Communist political parties. Then, on May 2, Hungary took down the barbed-wire fence that had long snaked along the Hungarian–Austrian border. For the first time since the 1940s, a Warsaw Pact country was opening up its border with the West![8]

When the government's big May Day (May 1) celebration drew a much smaller crowd than a competing opposition rally, the message was clear even to the Communist authorities. "The Communists are finished," one party official admitted that same night.[9] A week later, the party's longtime leader,

Janos Kadar, was forced to retire. In June, the party named a four-person presidium to rule the country temporarily while a new form of government was being worked out.[10] The temporary government soon entered into negotiations with some of the more than fifty opposition parties that had sprung up around the country. They agreed to hold elections that would end one-party control of Hungary, beginning in March 1990. Later in the year, the Workers' Guard, the militia the Hungarian Communist party had used to enforce its will, was disbanded.

The party did its best to position itself for the upcoming elections. At a party congress in October, the Communists did everything they could to distance themselves from their past. The party formally renounced Marxism and officially changed its name to the Hungarian Socialist party. It announced that it planned to move Hungary toward both a free market economy and a multiparty democratic system. On October 23, it proclaimed Hungary a free and independent republic.

The party's repositioning did it little good. When the elections were finally held in March and April, the Communists were thrown out. The election was won by a conservative coalition that was led by a party calling itself the Hungarian Democratic Forum.

THE WALL COMES TUMBLING DOWN IN EAST GERMANY

The opening of the border between Hungary and Austria was the beginning of the end of the Berlin Wall. The purpose of the wall, after all, was to keep East Germans from escaping to the greater freedom and economic opportunity of the West. But East German citizens were still free to cross into their Warsaw Pact neighbor, Czechoslovakia. From there, they could easily cross over into Hungary. And once Hungary's western border was open, they were free to go from Hungary into Austria—and so to freedom.

Thousands upon thousands of East Germans did just that. By late September, as many as two or three thousand a day were pouring into Austria. The government had travel restrictions in effect, but as long as the borders remained open at all, it was impossible to enforce them. There was no way to read the minds of people crossing the border, to find out whether they intended to come back.

The only way to stop the exodus would have been to close *all* of East Germany's borders. That would have meant isolating East Germany almost entirely from the outside world. Since the government had neither the manpower nor the will to take that drastic step, it was forced to stand by and watch as thousands of its citizens fled the country.

The Communist government, led by an aging Communist named Erich Honecker, wouldn't have minded if only the elderly and the disabled were leaving. They were an economic burden on the state. But once again, just as in 1961, it was mostly the skilled and well-educated who were heading west, in search of better jobs and higher pay. The East German economy was in fairly good shape as Eastern European economies went, but it was still behind most western European nations in what it could offer its people in pay and availability of consumer goods.

The continuing exodus was embarrassing to the East German government. It was graphic proof that, despite its relative economic success, it had failed to provide a satisfying life for its citizens. Even worse than the embarrassment to the government was the damage the exodus was doing to the economy. East Germany was losing its most valuable resource: its best and most-educated workers.

East Germany celebrated its fortieth birthday in October 1989. It had no idea, even then, that it would be the last celebration of a divided German state. Mikhail Gorbachev came from the Societ Union to join the celebration and to publicly embrace Honecker. He advised the East German people not to panic. Privately, it is likely that Gorbachev advised Honecker to do what so many other Eastern European leaders had already done: to undertake reforms.[11] If so, Honecker apparently refused to listen. He was among the most ideologically committed—and the most stubborn—of the old-line Communists in Europe.

The government tried to put the best face on the exodus by claiming that many of the refugees were not leaving of their own free will at all—they were being deported. But no one, inside or outside East Germany, really believed that.

The next development seemed inevitable. On October 18, Honecker was forced out as leader of East Germany. He was replaced by Egon Krenz. Krenz was yet another committed Communist, but he was a younger man who was open to at least some amount of reform.

On November 9, the Krenz government opened the border with West Germany. For the first time since 1961, East Germans were free to emigrate. The Berlin Wall came tumbling down. The government's reasoning was simple but desperate. If people knew that they were free to leave East Germany at any time, they might not actually go. Or if they did go, they might only visit briefly, and then they might come back.

Two hundred thousand East Germans poured out of the country in the remaining two months of 1989,[12] and 200,000 more left in the first two months of 1990.[13] And many thousands of them took their best possessions with them. They had no intention of coming back.

Although Krenz opened the border *and* promised economic reforms and free elections, he never really won the trust of the East German people. In the public mind he was tied too closely to communism and to the old regime of Erich Honecker. Shortly after Krenz took office, a scandal broke, revealing widespread corruption in the old Honecker regime. The scandal only added to the general distrust of Krenz.

Huge demonstrations in Berlin and Leipzig called for Krenz's ouster. In early December, after only six weeks in office, he and the entire leadership of the Communist party resigned. At the same time, the ex-president, Erich Honecker, was formally expelled from the Communist party he had once led. Gregor Gysi, a committed Communist but one known for his defense of dissidents, was made the new leader of the party, and Hans Modrow was named prime minister.

In early 1990, Modrow made the mistake of proposing a new secret police force to replace the hated Stasi that had long terrorized the population under Honecker. The resulting outcry against him led him to open up his government to non-Communist opposition leaders. He appointed several of them to serve in his cabinet.[14] So it was essentially a coalition government, dominated by reform Communists, that prepared for the first free elections in East German history.

The elections, held on March 18, 1990, gave a resounding victory to the opposition parties. The Communist party, which had renamed itself the Party of Democratic Socialism, got only 16 percent of the votes and just 65 of the 400 seats in the East German parliament. The big winner was a conservative coalition that called itself the Christian Democrat alliance.

Winning almost half of the votes (48 percent) and 193 of the seats, it was able to dominate the parliament and form a government. The alliance chose Lothar de Maizière, a respected lawyer with a background in religion and classical music as well as in law, to be prime minister.

In local elections held later in the year, the Social Democrats did better. So did the Greens, a party devoted to ecological reforms. But Christian Democrats were now in charge of the national government of East Germany. In the election campaign, they had proclaimed themselves in favor of the reunification of the two Germanies, and their victory was seen as a vote in favor of union. "Our first [job]," declared de Maizière, "will be to deal with unification and the economy, to convince people to stay here."[15] Ironically, the only way to keep people in East Germany would be to do away with East Germany altogether.

CZECHOSLOVAKIA STAGES A "VELVET REVOLUTION"

The Husak regime in Czechoslovakia resisted the revolutionary changes taking place elsewhere in Eastern Europe. Instead of bending to demands for liberalization, it responded by cracking down on those who called for reform. Leading dissidents were arrested and jailed for short periods of time. Among them was a popular playwright named Vaclav Havel.

But by the fall of 1989, the Czechoslovakians were getting more and more restless. On November 17, 1989, thousands of people, many of them university students, took to the streets of Prague. It was the biggest demonstration in Czechoslovakia since a demonstration mourning the end of the Prague Spring took place in August 1969.

The Prague demonstration had supposedly been

called to commemorate the killing of a student by the Nazis during World War II, but it quickly turned into a rally against the Communist government. "Dinosaurs, resign!" the students shouted. "Communists, get out!"[16] When the demonstrators attempted to march through the city, they were attacked by riot police. Tear gas was fired into the crowd. Hundreds of demonstrators were beaten, and at least thirteen were later admitted to hospitals. Scores of the demonstrators were arrested.

The violence against them failed to intimidate the dissidents. If anything, it enraged and encouraged them. Two days later, they held another demonstration. It was around this time that a dissident civil rights group called Charta 77 re-formed itself into a political party called Civic Forum. Among the founders of both was Vaclav Havel, who had been freed from prison after a public outcry earlier in the year.

Civic Forum, which was a largely Czech organization, was soon joined by a similar Slovak group calling itself Public Against Violence. Inspired by these and other opposition groups, 200,000 people gathered in Prague on November 20 for the biggest demonstration yet. That same day, thousands of other Czechoslovakians swept through the boulevards and squares of other cities throughout the country.

Four days later, Alexander Dubček, the man who had led the reforms of 1968, appeared at an even bigger rally in Prague. Some 500,000 people jammed Wenceslaus Square, cheering as Dubček called for the downfall of the Communist government led by Miloš Jakes. Jakes resigned later that same day.[17] On November 27, millions of Czechoslovak workers took part in a general strike to demonstrate their opposition to the government.

On December 4, the Soviet Union led the Warsaw Pact in a joint declaration of regret for their invasion of Czechoslovakia in 1968. The Brezhnev Doctrine was officially dead.[18]

By this time the Czechoslovak Communist party knew it could no longer stay in power. It no longer had the support or commanded the fear of the people, and it was clear that the Soviet Union would not step in to save it. On the twenty-ninth, the Czechoslovak Parliament, despite its large majority of Communists, voted to repeal Article 4 of the constitution—the article that guaranteed the Communist party a leading role in the government.[19]

Negotiations between the government and the opposition led to a coalition that would run the country until elections took place sometime in 1990. The new coalition was dominated by non-Communists and led by Vaclav Havel, who was named president of the coalition government. He referred to what had taken place in Czechoslovakia as a "velvet revolution," apparently a reference to an American rock group called the Velvet Underground.

The elections were held in June 1990. Civic Forum and Public Against Violence won 170 of the 300 seats in the parliament. The Communists came in second, taking 47 seats, and a third, non-Communist party, known as the Christian Democrats, took 40. Three smaller parties, representing basically regional interests, took the remaining few seats.[20]

THE EX-COMMUNISTS WIN IN BULGARIA

For four decades, the people of Bulgaria had accepted their one-party state. They might not have been happy with their hard-line Communist government, but they were exceptionally docile and obedient to it, even by the repressed standards of Eastern Europe.

There were some dissidents in Bulgaria, but they seemed to be relatively isolated, and they received little obvious support from the masses of the Bulgarian people.

The public challenges that Poland threw out to Soviet domination had no echoes in Bulgaria. When Hungary exploded in 1956, Bulgaria stayed eerily quiet. When Czechoslovakian freedom flowered during the sunny spring of 1968, Bulgaria remained gloomy and dark. During all of that time, there was not one large public protest against the government.

But finally, in November 1989, 4,000 Bulgarians took to the streets of Sofia, the capital. The long silence was over. People were beginning to demand democracy. They had had enough of one-party government and of Todor Zhivkov, who had ruled as the virtual dictator of Bulgaria for thirty-five years. They wanted change. And just as it had come in so many other places during that remarkable year, change came suddenly and with surprising ease. On November 10, just days after the first demonstration, the seemingly immovable Todor Zhivkov resigned.

Zhivkov's successor, Petar Mladenov, acknowledged that change was needed. "Real power," he said, "[has] to be given to the people."[21] The people seemed to agree. Tens of thousands of them flooded into the streets, calling for democracy and demanding an end to police brutality and political repression. On December 12, Mladenov promised to take away the Communist party's special status and to hold free elections the following June.[22] In preparation for those elections, the party changed its name to the Bulgarian Socialist party.

In February 1990, the government was reorganized. Mladenov was replaced as the head of the party, and Andrei Lukanov was chosen as prime minister. Lukanov had also been a Communist, but he promised to work in cooperation with the opposition in the months leading up to the elections.[23]

Most people expected the promised elections, which took place in two rounds that June, to follow the pattern set in the other countries of Eastern Europe. That is, they expected that the Bulgarian Socialist party would suffer a humiliating defeat and that the coalition, Union of Democratic Forces, would win. But the results of the opening round of elections showed that just the opposite was happening. The Bulgarian Socialist party, led by Mladenov, won 107 seats in that round, compared to only 40 for all opposition parties.[24] By the time the second round was over, the once Communist party had won a landslide victory and the great majority of the 400 seats in the Bulgarian parliament.

Supporters of the Union of Democratic Forces were so staggered by the results they refused to accept them. They took to the streets in protest. They insisted the elections had been rigged. They *had* to be. How could the Communists win an honest election? But they had. Official observers from several countries, who had come to Bulgaria to watch the election process, insisted that it had been fair. A British observer told a reporter for America's National Public Radio that it would have been as hard to fix the Bulgarian election as to fix an election in Britain itself. The Bulgarian Socialist party's victory was just one more surprise in a year of surprises.

The Union of Democratic Forces, however, was not satisfied to accept the results of the election. Supporters continued to protest the past actions of the victors. That summer, some 30,000 demonstrators set up a tent city, camping in to protest the government. They demanded the president resign because he had approved the use of tanks to break up a demonstration the previous December. Bowing to the pressure,

Mladenov stepped down as president, "in order not to . . . increase political tensions."[25]

The demonstrators rejoiced, but they were far from satisfied. They continued to press for other demands: for a public trial of the ex-dictator Zhivkov and for a full accounting of the finances of the ex-Communists in the government. They believed that many, if not all, of the major officials had used their offices to profit at the expense of the Bulgarian people.[26]

"Never again a Communist president in Bulgaria!" cried one of the demonstrators, addressing the crowd. In that, too, the protesters got their wish, at least for the time being. An opposition leader, Zhelyu Zhelov, was chosen to replace Mladenov. But even so, the Bulgarian Parliament remains in the hands of the Bulgarian Socialist party. And so far, unlike what has happened in the other newly democratic nations of Eastern Europe, the ex-Communists have been able to block any real revelation of the abuses and crimes of the previous government.

9
THE BLOODBATH IN THE STREETS OF ROMANIA

One of the most remarkable things about the revolutionary changes that took place in 1989 was how little violence there was. Revolutions are usually bloody events, filled with armed clashes, assassinations, and massacres. But in Poland, Hungary, Bulgaria, East Germany, and even in Czechoslovakia, there had been none of those.

That is not to say that there was no violence at all. In most of the countries, the secret police harassed dissidents and those suspected of supporting dissidents. Some were jailed. Some were tortured. Some disappeared. But these were usually isolated, if not rare, events.

In several of the countries, there were demonstrations that got out of hand. Some were put down by brutal and clearly excessive force. But the violence on both sides was contained. Although there were many wounds, there were few life-threatening injuries and even fewer deaths. Andrei Sakharov was not strictly accurate in describing the events in Eastern

Europe as "bloodless revolutions," but the essence of what he said was true—except in one country.

Except in Romania.

Romania was the exception that proved the rule. What happened there made clear the tragedy that the other countries of Eastern Europe had escaped. For in Romania, although it was brief, the revolution was incredibly violent, brutal, and merciless—on both sides.

THE ECCENTRIC DICTATOR

Romania had been something of an oddity in Eastern Europe ever since its president, Nicolae Ceauşescu, had taken dictatorial power in 1965. Ceauşescu considered himself to be a hard-line, traditional Communist. In a sense he was, if the model for a hard-line, traditional Communist was Joseph Stalin.

But compared to the heads of most of the Eastern European governments, Ceauşescu was extremely eccentric. Some even said he was insane. He had a very personal vision of the ideal of a Communist state, and he was determined to build that state in Romania. To do so, he was prepared to tear down the Romania that already existed and rebuild it according to his own plan.

He literally set out to level the thousands of small towns that formed the structure of his largely rural country. In their place, he built prefabricated urban-agricultural centers, in which he forced the peasants whose homes he had destroyed to live.

Another aspect of his vision required the creation of an ethnically pure nation out of his ethnically mixed state. He forced German and Hungarian ethnic minorities who lived in the country to give up their cultural identities and to become virtually indistinguishable from other Romanians. Romanian Jews, who were less willing to give up their traditions, were sold exit visas to Israel. To build up the ethnic Romanian population, he forbade women who had not already had at least four (and later five) children to practice birth control.

With his wife and other members of his family, he ruled Romania as a strange mixture of a Communist state and a private kingdom. Ceauşescu's orders were enforced by the 180,000-strong Securitate, a secret police force loyal only to the Ceauşescu family.[1] It was considered the most powerful, and hated, in all of Eastern Europe, even worse than the dreaded Stasi in East Germany.

With the Securitate firmly behind him, Ceauşescu seemed to be in safe and total control of Romania. He scoffed at demands for change and even scolded Mikhail Gorbachev for what he considered the watering down of communism in the Soviet Union. Even when the other Eastern European regimes began toppling all around him, most foreign observers were sure his regime would survive. As 1989 drew to a close, there was still no sign that Romania was vulnerable to the changes that were sweeping Eastern Europe.

If anything, Ceauşescu seemed stronger than ever. On November 24, a congress of the Romanian Communist party reelected him as its chief with not one dissenting vote. Ceauşescu used the opportunity to once again denounce all talk of reform. Other leaders might weaken and compromise, but he would continue to follow his "golden dream of communism."[2]

THE REVOLUTION BEGINS

Less than a month later, dissidents launched a demonstration in the city of Timisoara in western Romania. They were protesting a plan to deport an ethnic

114

Hungarian clergyman who had spoken out against the Ceauşescu government. The demonstrators formed a human chain to protect the minister. It isn't clear how it began, but violence broke out. Before long, the relatively small and isolated protest turned into a series of mass demonstrations against the government.

On December 16, Securitate and army troops were ordered to fire on the demonstrators. In the slaughter that followed, thousands of Romanian citizens were shot. The government tried to impose a news blackout, but word leaked out that thousands of people had died. There were sensational reports of a mass grave, into which 4,500 bodies had been thrown.

It later turned out that the mass grave had actually been an old paupers' cemetery.[3] But many of the other stories of government brutality were true. Certainly hundreds, perhaps over a thousand, people had died. The official figure later announced by the government that took over after the revolution was 689.[4] As word of events in Timisoara spread, people around the country began taking to the streets to protest the government.

THE ARMY SIDES WITH THE PEOPLE

Some of the army troops refused to take action against their own people, no matter what the government or the Securitate wanted. An eyewitness later described one such incident to CNN Television news: "I saw soldiers facing a woman. A [Securitate agent] ordered them to shoot the woman. The soldiers refused. They threw down their guns. . . . The [Securitate agent] shot the soldiers."[5]

Eventually, this kind of spontaneous split between the army troops and the Securitate became official. The army generals had always resented Securitate power anyway. Now, with antigovernment violence spreading throughout Romania, they ordered their troops to side with the people and against Ceauşescu's security police.

For almost a week, the bloody civil war raged on in Romania. Ceauşescu did not seem to believe what was happening. He ordered a progovernment rally held in the capital of Bucharest. When a crowd dutifully gathered in front of the presidential palace, Ceauşescu addressed them. He blamed the violence on ethnic Hungarians who wanted Transylvania returned to Hungary.[6] Blaming trouble on Hungarians usually got a positive response from a Romanian crowd. But not this time. This time Ceauşescu was booed. Alarmed and angered, he stormed into the palace. It was the last time he would ever be seen in public.

When it became clear that the Securitate *could* not protect him, and the army *would* not, Ceauşescu and his wife Elena went into hiding. They were captured by the revolutionaries on December 24. They were immediately tried for treason in a mockery of a trial that took less than a day. They didn't even bother to defend themselves. They insisted that the "court" had no right to try them. On Christmas Day, they were convicted and condemned to death. Fifteen minutes later, believing they were on their way to a prison cell, they were shot dead.[7]

THE NATIONAL SALVATION FRONT

The execution of the Ceauşescus brought a quick and victorious end to the revolution. A provisional government was hastily set up by a group calling itself the National Salvation Front, headed by an ex-government figure named Ion Iliescu.

116

The new government was controversial from the start. Although Iliescu was known as an enemy of Ceauşescu and was personally widely respected, he had also been a Communist. Many anti-Communists who had participated in the civil war complained that their revolution had been co-opted (or stolen) by the Communists.

Iliescu tried to calm their fears. He promised reforms and free elections. He spoke of a coalition government that would turn Romania into a social democracy, along the lines of Sweden. When the promised elections were held in May, the National Salvation Front won in a landslide. As in Bulgaria, the opposition insisted that the election had been rigged. But once again, the foreign observers disagreed. Although some had witnessed questionable practices that probably increased the government's totals, they conceded that the elections had been generally fair. There could be no real question that the National Salvation Front had won it.[8]

Even so, protests continued. One, in University Square in Bucharest, went on for fifty-three days. At the end of that time, riot troops moved in and forcibly cleared the square. When protesters later raided and firebombed government buildings, Iliescu appealed to the nation's coal miners, who strongly supported the new regime, to come to Bucharest. They came by the truckload, brandishing iron bars and yelling, "The workers are here!" Police stood by as they swept through the city, beating up and intimidating the dissidents.[9]

Because of the repression that was used to quell the demonstrations, diplomats boycotted the inauguration of Iliescu, even though he was the first freely elected president of Romania since long before World War II.[10] Clearly, Romania's current government is better than the eccentric dictatorship of Nicolae

Ceaușescu. But many observers, both inside and outside Romania, complain that Romania's government is still more like the old-line governments of Eastern Europe than it is like those of Romania's newly democratic neighbors. They lament what has been called Romania's "phony revolution."

Whatever the faults of Ion Iliescu's government, it had been elected by the people of Romania. And Romania was the last of the countries of Eastern Europe to hold a free election. Within a few dizzying months, Poland, Czechoslovakia, Hungary, Bulgaria, East Germany, and then Romania had all gone through astounding and historic transformations. Each had moved, in its own way, from an imposed government to a freely chosen one.

The new governments were as different as the countries themselves. Some, like the one in Poland, seemed determined to rush headlong into reform. Some, like the one in Czechoslovakia, seemed much more cautious. Some, like those in Poland and Czechoslovakia, seemed extremely idealistic, even naive. Some, like the one in Romania, seemed just the opposite. At least one, that of East Germany, seemed ready to abolish itself altogether.

But how these governments turned out—whether they would be good or bad, whether they would succeed or fail—mattered less than the fact that they existed at all.

Against all odds, and with amazing suddenness, democracy had come to Eastern Europe.

118

10
THREE CHALLENGES FACING EASTERN EUROPE

The events of 1989 were so unexpected and so full of promise that they seemed almost miraculous. Throughout Eastern Europe, people rejoiced at throwing off decades of oppression. But once the first intoxication of sudden freedom had passed, the countries of Eastern Europe had to face up to some sobering realities.

An enormous burden—the burden of Soviet Communist domination—was now lifted from their shoulders. But many other problems remained. They would have to take stock of themselves and look to the future.

They had their independence, but what were they going to do with it?

The new Eastern Europe will face a series of difficult challenges in the next decade. Each of those challenges holds out enormous promise for the future, and each is filled with enormous potential danger—for Eastern Europe and the world.

119

1. MOVING FROM COMMUNISM TO CAPITALISM

Four decades of communism have left many of the countries of Eastern Europe struggling for economic survival.

Most of their factories are outdated. Even those businesses that are relatively modern are inefficient. Trying to provide jobs for everyone, the old Communist governments created thousands of busywork jobs that drained resources but added nothing of value to the national economies.

Most of the goods produced in Eastern Europe are notoriously shoddy. They are so inferior to those made elsewhere that they cannot be exported or sold on the open market. No one wants to buy them. The only large foreign market many of them had was the Soviet Union, which bought them mainly as a favor to its allies. Now even the Soviet Union has cut back on its purchases of Eastern European goods.

The lack of foreign markets has left the countries of Eastern Europe low on foreign currency. The little they do have has to go to pay off debts they owe to other countries. Poland and Hungary, in particular, are saddled with billions of dollars in foreign debt. The problem is made worse by the fact that foreign nations will not take payment for their goods in Eastern European currency. The lack of foreign currency means that there is little available to purchase foreign-made goods, from such necessities as food and fuel to luxury items like television sets and toilet paper. Shortages of all of these things are common.

Most of the new governments believe that the cure for their economic problems lies in the domains of capitalism and free enterprise. With the exception of Bulgaria and Romania, they have already prescribed large doses of these remedies for themselves. Czechoslovakia has announced that it will allow the creation of more private property, and it has begun taking steps to establish a market economy. Hungary, which had already flirted with capitalism long before its change of government, is encouraging even more private enterprise. East Germany, which has merged with West Germany, hopes to blend its economy entirely into the capitalist economy of West Germany.

Most of these countries are encouraging foreign investment. Drawn by a cheap work force, several companies from Japan, the United States, and Western Europe had already begun operations in Eastern Europe even before 1989.[1] Hungary in particular had been especially active, and successful, in attracting Western companies. Now other Eastern European countries are following Hungary's lead.

So far, however, most of the progress toward capitalism has been timid. Living under communism, the people of Eastern Europe have grown used to having their economic lives run by the government. Many are uneasy about being cast out on their own. Relying on the government may have resulted in a low standard of living and restricted their freedom, but it was safe. The quality of the health care, welfare, and other social services the people received was poor, but at least it was free. The jobs they had paid poorly, but they were secure. The businesses they worked in were wasteful and unproductive, but they never failed (the government always kept them going, no matter what). The goods that people could buy were shoddy and scarce, but the prices were low.

Under capitalism, all of this is bound to change. And at first, the change will be for the worse. Inefficient businesses will shut down. Jobs will be lost. Prices will rise according to market forces the government cannot control. All of these are strange and frightening possibilities for people—and political leaders—who have known nothing but communism for generations.

Of all the countries of Eastern Europe, Poland was the only one to dive headfirst into the icy waters of capitalism. In December 1989, the Solidarity government instituted the most sweeping and radical economic reforms seen in Eastern Europe since the introduction of communism itself.

Virtually overnight, the government cut subsidies to industry in half. Prices of coal and other energy sources (which had been kept artificially low) were allowed to rise by 500 percent to 700 percent. Many other prices were also allowed to rise, while wage increases were severely limited. Tax laws and policies for granting credit to industries were toughened.[2]

In the long run, the government hopes that this "shock therapy" will force the Polish economy to become more efficient, make Polish industry more productive, and provide more jobs. But in the short term, it is bound to cause many industries to fail, resulting in the loss of many jobs. In addition, it is expected to cause an immediate reduction in the total output of the Polish economy and a 20 percent drop in the already low incomes of ordinary Poles.[3] In fact, within a few weeks of the reform, 70,000 small businesses had already collapsed in Poland.[4]

Many Poles are not sure the painful experiment is worth it. One Polish farmer, interviewed for the Public Broadcasting System program "Frontline," expressed the confusion many Poles feel when faced with the uncertainties of an unplanned capitalist economy. "One [person] pays more. The other pays less. Today more. Tomorrow less. This free price system is a mess. We are going crazy."[5]

Still, by the spring of 1990, the economic situation in Poland showed some signs of improving. Inflation (the rise in the prices consumers pay for goods) dropped to 70 percent in January, and to 24 percent in February.[6] These are still very high inflation rates but nowhere near the 700 percent inflation that was raging in 1989.

If more improvements occur, and if they occur fast enough, there is real hope that Poland's "shock therapy" may serve as a model for others. But it is still too early to tell whether the experiment will succeed. And even if it does, it is possible that no other government will dare to copy it.

Except for Vaclav Havel, who heads Czechoslovakia's new government, none of the other political leaders in Eastern Europe enjoys the kind of public faith and goodwill that Solidarity enjoys. And without the Polish people's willingness to give Solidarity and Lech Walesa a chance to prove themselves, they would never have accepted such painful reforms. In any other country in Eastern Europe, the same measures probably would have caused a revolt. Even in Poland, there have been several strikes to protest the effects of the government's drastic policies.

It is not surprising that the countries of Eastern Europe are having trouble taking the plunge into capitalism. What they are attempting has never been done before. No country has ever successfully moved from a Communist system to a capitalist system. Since communism grew up as a response to capitalism, all of the movement has been the other way. As one Soviet economist has pointed out, "We have written and read many books on how to turn capitalism into socialism, but we have no books to tell us how to turn socialism into capitalism."[7]

2. ADJUSTING TO DEMOCRACY

The American Constitutional Convention was held in secret. It is said that at the end of it, a citizen who had not been present at the convention approached one of the Founding Fathers. "Well," he asked, "what kind of government do I have?"

"A republic, sir," the Founding Father answered, "if you can keep it."

For a citizen of Eastern Europe today, the answer would be "a democracy, sir, if you can keep it." A democracy is not an easy thing to keep, particularly for those who have no tradition of democratic practices. And real democracy is as foreign to the people of Eastern Europe today as capitalism is. They have no ongoing tradition of independent political parties or contested elections, much less of free speech and tolerance for dissent.

The last time these countries were independent, all except Czechoslovakia fell into the clutches of right-wing, authoritarian, and antidemocratic regimes. There is a real risk that they will do so again. The people of these countries are used to having one party (or one person) in total control. Already there are complaints in Poland that people are relying too much on the personal leadership of Lech Walesa. And in Czechoslovakia, there are reports that President Vaclav Havel might be becoming too popular. Havel himself has commented on the problem. He says he's afraid to say that he doesn't like a dog he sees in the street. If he does, he complains jokingly, there will be five people with guns ready to shoot the dog for him.[8]

Havel and Walesa both seem to be true democrats, but the tendency to develop a "cult of personality" around them is disturbing. When people put their leaders on pedestals, they often hand them too much power. That is a tendency that has caused a lot of trouble in Eastern Europe in the past.

Most of the people who live in the region today were raised in one-party dictatorships. They are not used to the art of compromise, nor to playing by political rules—two essentials of democratic systems. Even the most pro-democratic forces in some of the countries do not seem to understand how democracy

124

operates. When the anti-Communist forces lost the May 1990 elections in Bulgaria, for instance, their response was to take to the streets and try to force the resignation of the freely elected president.

One of the hardest challenges for any democracy is protecting the interests and the rights of minorities. Since decisions are made by the majority, the interests of religious, ethnic, racial, and other minorities can easily be ignored. The Western democracies have established traditions of not only accepting but of protecting minority rights. (In the United States we have the Constitution with its Bill of Rights.) But even in the West, it is a constant struggle to see that those rights remain protected.

Eastern Europe, on the other hand, has a less tolerant tradition. For example, publicly endorsed anti-Semitism (prejudice against Jews) has a long history there. Anti-Semitism was so strong, in fact, that many citizens in Romania, Poland, and elsewhere were willing to fall in with the Nazis' attempt to wipe out the Jews in Europe during World War II. Because of the Nazis, in fact, there are relatively few Jews left in any of these countries. The number of Jews in Poland, for example, plunged from 3,300,000 before the war to a mere 4,400 today. Even Hungary, which has the most, has only 60,000 to 80,000 Jewish citizens today, compared to over 400,000 who lived there before the war. Even today there is still a tendency among some elements of Eastern European society to blame the Jews for many of the problems that plague the area.[9]

All of these countries have large minority populations. Romania, for example, has over 1 million Hungarians and Transylvanians, most of whom also belong to the minority Roman Catholic religion. Bulgaria has some 800,000 Turks, most of whom are Muslims. About 31 percent of all Czechoslovakians are

125

Slovaks, whereas the majority are Czechs. Each country also has significant numbers of Gypsies and other smaller minority groups. Virtually all of these minorities have suffered from long histories of discrimination inside their countries, and all are worried about their futures under the new regimes.

Their presence, and the widespread prejudice against them, will put severe strains on the new democratic political systems. How will these minority populations be represented in the government? How will their rights be protected against the prejudice or indifference of the majority?

In the end, it may be as hard for the people of Eastern Europe to adjust to the compromises of democracy as it will be to adjust to free markets and private enterprise.

3. CLEANING UP THE ENVIRONMENT

Taken as a whole, Eastern Europe is probably the most polluted region on earth. In the desperate effort to make their centralized economies productive, the Communist governments ignored the environment. They allowed coal-burning power plants to spew carbon monoxide, ash, and other pollutants into the air. They allowed factories to pour oceans of waste chemicals into the waterways. They disposed of their hazardous wastes in the cheapest ways possible, often just piling them up in dumps, where toxic fumes could escape into the air and acids and other poisons could soak into the earth, contaminating the soil and eventually seeping into the groundwater underneath.

Even in recent decades, when scientists around the world were warning against acid rain, global warming, and the greenhouse effect, these governments did nothing to end the polluting of their air, land, and water. Industries continued to operate without effective environmental regulations, often without any emission controls at all.

The result has been an environmental disaster. Over a vast industrial region that cuts across Eastern Europe from the southern section of East Germany, through Czechoslovakia, and into Poland, almost 40 percent of the forests have been damaged by acid rain. In parts of this area, *all* of the trees have been killed, stripped of their leaves by chemicals in the very rainwater that should have brought them nourishment and life. Half of the drinking water in Czechoslovakia is contaminated. More than 90 percent of the river water in Poland and Romania is too polluted to drink. The once beautiful "blue Danube," the river that flows through Hungary, Poland, and Romania has become a toxic soup. A whole section of Bilina, Czechoslovakia, is a ghost town because contaminants from nearby industries have made it impossible to live there. The Romanian town of Copsa Mica has become infamous as the "black town" because the tons of factory soot that are spewed into the air each day cover everything with a layer of black filth. All across Eastern Europe, large numbers of people are dying painful deaths from pollution-related diseases.[10]

In some of the Eastern European countries, including Bulgaria, public anger at what was happening to the environment helped fuel the demand for changes in the political system. Now it is up to the new governments of Eastern Europe to clean up the great poisonous mess their countries have made of their environments.

Sadly, no one thinks they can do it. They do not even have the resources to retool their factories in order to stop polluting in the future, much less to repair the damage that has been done in the past.

Meanwhile, the environment that is still being contaminated is not confined to Eastern Europe. The

127

movements of air and water are not restricted by borders. Rivers eventually make their way to the sea. The poisons that rise into the air in one country can come down in another. The atmosphere they contaminate and the earth-protecting ozone layer they damage are shared by people around the world.

Recognizing this, some other countries have begun to help. West Germany has sent $500 million to help in East Germany, and Sweden has offered $45 million to help in Poland. But these amounts are pitifully small compared to the size of the problem. One study suggests that $200 billion may be necessary just to deal with industrial pollution alone.

Eastern Europeans are not the only ones who have to take stock of the changes that have been—and still are—taking place in the region. Thanks to the momentous events of 1989, the world is going to be a very different place from what it was before.

A whole new set of realities now faces not just Eastern Europe but western Europe, the Soviet Union, and the United States as well. Some of the new realities are immediately obvious. Others are just beginning to come into focus. Still others may not become apparent for several years.

In the concluding chapter we will look at a few of the challenges that now face the rest of the world as a result of the changes in Eastern Europe.

11
THE POST–COLD WAR WORLD

The greatest challenge facing the United States, and the West in general, will be understanding what the events in Eastern Europe mean for the future. Old policies that have been refined for decades will have to be abandoned, as the world adjusts to the new realities. And the hardest new reality to adjust to may be the end of the cold war.

THE END OF THE COLD WAR

The cold war has been the central fact of life of international relations for forty years. Both American and Soviet foreign policy have been largely based on the threat that each of them has presented to the other. Most of the countries of Europe were tied to one or the other of the superpowers, through either NATO or the Warsaw Pact. Both camps lived with the constant threat of a military conflict between them that could throw the world into nuclear war.

Suddenly, that threat is greatly reduced—if not entirely eliminated. By the time the Berlin Wall came down, even hard-line cold warriors were admitting that the cold war seemed to be ending. One of them was Jeane Kirkpatrick, who had served as U.S. ambassador to the United Nations during the early days of the Reagan administration. "It's been clear for quite some time," she told a newspaper interviewer at the time, "that the post–World War II era was coming to an end." The destruction of the wall, she said, "dramatized that ending in a fantastic and unexpected way."[1]

The cold war was an expensive, dangerous, and exhausting struggle. People on both sides greeted its end with great joy. In the West, there was a sense of satisfaction as well as of relief: not only was the war over, the political leaders said, but the West had won. The Western ideals of democracy, personal liberty, and economic freedom had triumphed over the Soviet Union's brand of repressive communism.

But however welcome the changes are, adjusting to them will not be easy. The new world situation requires new ways of looking at the world. Nations that have lived in the dark shadow of the cold war for forty years will have to become accustomed to the sunlight. As the 1990s move on, governments and peoples on both sides of the vanished iron curtain will struggle to understand what the end of the cold war will mean to them—and to the future of the world.

The first effects of the end of the cold war were seen in the Warsaw Pact. As early as the summer of 1990, it was clear that the alliance was collapsing. No one believed that the new governments of Eastern Europe would send troops into battle at the request of the Soviet Union. And Soviet troops were already pulling out of some of the Eastern European countries in which they had been stationed for decades.

130

The collapse of the Warsaw Pact was welcomed by the West, but it raised serious questions about the West's own alliances. With the Warsaw Pact falling apart, what will be the future of NATO? A Soviet spokesman, Gennady Gerasimov, questions the reason for NATO's very existence. "NATO has no enemy anymore," he declared.[2] By the time the NATO nations met in London in July 1990, even many NATO leaders were beginning to agree with him. At that meeting, NATO announced a new era of peaceful cooperation between its members and the members of the Warsaw Pact. It offered to sign nonaggression pacts with the nations of Eastern Europe and even invited Mikhail Gorbachev to address a future NATO meeting.[3]

The offers of cooperation and peace that came out of the NATO meeting suggest the great promise of a post–cold war future, but there may be dangers lurking in that future, too. The long, dangerous confrontation between NATO and the Warsaw Treaty Organization has had its benefits as well as its terrors. The cold war kept a kind of peace on the continent of Europe for forty years. However uneasy and uncomfortable it may have been, that was the longest period of peace that Europe had seen in centuries.

Time and again, in the years before the cold war, the countries of Europe had fallen into quarrels among themselves. Those quarrels had often led to war. Twice, in the twentieth century alone, conflicts in Eastern Europe sparked major wars that engulfed the world. But in the decades since the end of World War II, the two great alliances of NATO and the Warsaw Pact managed to keep such national quarrels in check. What will keep them in check now, with the cold war over and the two alliances on the verge of breaking up?

THE NUCLEAR THREAT

At least as troubling is the question of nuclear war. Despite the constant threat of nuclear confrontation, the cold war also managed to keep the nuclear peace. Neither side dared to use the terrible weapons. Although other countries had developed their own nuclear weapons, no one else had used them either.

To some extent at least, the reluctance to use these weapons was a result of the balance of terror between the superpowers. Everyone feared that the use of nuclear weapons *anywhere* might somehow trigger an all-out, world-destroying nuclear exchange between the Soviet Union and the United States. With that threat lessened, there is at least the danger that some countries might be more tempted to use nuclear weapons to settle their own disputes. Among those countries may be the United States itself. At one point in 1990, during the months leading up to the Persian Gulf War against Iraq, U.S. government spokespersons suggested that the United States would consider using "tactical nuclear weapons" if war actually broke out. Even though they were never used, the proposal was ominous.

A REUNIFIED GERMANY

If serious trouble breaks out on the continent of Europe, many people fear that it may be started by a reunified Germany. Until the Berlin Wall came down, no one talked very seriously about the reunification of the two Germanies. Even most Germans themselves, on both sides of the Wall, seemed to consider it a nonissue. Their two societies had become so different in the days since World War II that it was hard to imagine their ever merging.

Besides, there seemed to be no point in even

considering it. The Soviet Union, which still effectively controlled East Germany, opposed it. The countries of western Europe, who bitterly remembered Germany's role in two world wars, were frightened of it. Even if the Germans wanted it and pressed for it, it seemed certain that neither side in the cold war would allow it.

But when the Berlin Wall collapsed in late 1989, reunification suddenly began to seem possible—someday. It still seemed unlikely that it could happen any time soon. But within months, Lothar de Maizière and the Christian Democratic party, which had campaigned for reunification, were elected in East Germany. Now there were Christian Democratic and proreunification governments in *both* Germanies. The rapid merging of the two Germanies became not only likely but inevitable. Things moved ahead with blinding speed. Secret negotiations, known as the "2-plus-4 talks," prepared the groundwork for reunification. (The "2" were the two Germanies; the "4" were the Soviet Union, the United States, Great Britain, and France.) The first major step in the reunification process was taken on July 2, 1990, when the East German currency was abolished and both countries began using the stronger West German mark.

The two last obstacles to reunification were the question of German membership in NATO and the problem of Germany's long-disputed border with Poland—the so-called Oder-Neisse line.

West Germany, of course, had been a member of NATO; East Germany was a member of the Warsaw Pact. The United States insisted that a single Germany should take West Germany's old place in NATO. The Soviet Union said no. It would accept Germany not belonging to the Warsaw Pact only if it would not belong to NATO either. At one point in the discussions, Gorbachev suggested that the new Germany might, at

133

least for a while, belong to *both* NATO and the Warsaw Pact. But that suggestion was rejected.

The border between East Germany and Poland had been established by the victors after World War II. It had been accepted by the two Communist allies, but it had never been formally accepted by West Germany. Poland worried that a reunified Germany would challenge the border and demand some disputed territory that had been awarded to Poland after the war. Poland's fears increased when Germany refused to let Poland join the 2-plus-4 talks that were held to decide the issue.

Both problems were solved in mid-July 1990. In a historic negotiation between West German Chancellor Helmut Kohl and President Gorbachev, Gorbachev agreed that Germany could make up its own mind what alliances (if any) it would join. Since Kohl and de Maizère had already agreed that a united Germany should belong to NATO, Gorbachev was essentially accepting German membership in that alliance. That same week, West Germany announced that it would sign a treaty accepting the Oder-Neisse line.

German reunification, which had seemed an impossibility a year before, occurred in October 1990, only eleven months after the opening of the Berlin Wall.

Reunification is not an unmixed blessing for the Germans on either side of the now vanished border. As Horst Emhke of the German Parliament (known as the Bundestag) has put it, "We will pay a very high price in terms of social problems in the GDR, and financial problems in West Germany."[4] The one-time East Germans will struggle until they come up to the living standards of the West Germans, while the more prosperous West Germans will have to pay for the rebuilding of the East's depressed economy.

THE NEW GERMANY'S PLACE IN EUROPE

In essence, West Germany has absorbed East Germany. To the extent that Europe is still divided at all, Germany is now a part of western, not Eastern, Europe.

Meanwhile, the western European countries are moving toward a partial unification of their own. In 1992, the European Community plans to form a kind of United Europe. Each country will maintain its national identity, but most of the trade, economic, and cultural barriers between them will be removed. When that happens, the reunited Germany will be by far the biggest and strongest nation in the new Europe.

Economically, Germany will be not only the most important nation in western Europe but one of the most important in the entire world. It will, in fact, produce more per person than any other country except the United States and Japan.[5]

The development of a bigger and more powerful Germany is not an entirely happy thought for many Europeans who remember the German attempts to conquer Europe. Germany had been split up in the first place to keep it from ever being strong enough to challenge the rest of Europe again. Some people still feared that it was a mistake to allow it to reunify now.

Others tried to calm their fears. They pointed out that the Europe of the 1990s was not the same as the Europe of 1939, when World War II began. In those days, a storm of fascism was roaring across Europe. Today it is the refreshing wind of freedom that blows across the continent. Dominique Moise, a co-founder of the French Institute for International Relations, warns that "Nothing is more dangerous than to say to the Germans today, 'We fear you.' If we do that, we will create a Germany according to that image, the kind of Germany we would deserve."[6]

In any case, the reunified Germany is a fact—a fact the rest of the world will have to learn to live with.

THE FUTURE OF THE SOVIET UNION

Perhaps the biggest question mark in the future of Eastern Europe is what is going to happen inside the Soviet Union. The giant that once controlled all of Eastern Europe may soon be unable to control itself. Several of the very republics that make it up have grown rebellious. Independence movements have sprung up in republics all around the country.

The desire for independence is particularly strong in the Baltic republics of Estonia, Latvia, and Lithuania.[7] All three have declared their intention of becoming independent. In December 1989, Lithuania became the first to declare that it *was* independent and no longer a republic of the Soviet Union at all.[8] It eventually backed down (but only temporarily) when the Soviet Union cut off supplies of oil and other needed commodities to the defiant republic.

Unrest continued to plague the Baltics into 1991. In places, the Soviet army moved to stifle the protests against the national government. The harshness of the government crackdown in Lithuania shocked many Westerners who had thought that Gorbachev had moved beyond using such force against what he considered his own people. Some speculated that Gorbachev had not actually ordered the army actions at all. They suggested that the Soviet army might be getting out of control.

Early in 1991, Lithuania held a referendum in which a huge majority of voters chose independence.

The Soviet government declared the referendum illegal. Republics *could* leave the Soviet Union, Gorbachev insisted. But only if they followed the elaborate and time-consuming procedures set up under a new Soviet law. But those procedures seemed to be unacceptable to the leaders of Lithuania.

The Baltics were not alone either. Other trouble spots included the Republic of Azerbaijan, on the Soviet border with Iran. Fundamentalist Muslims, who wanted a union with their fellow fundamentalists across the Iranian border, launched a near revolution there in early 1990. Soviet troops were sent to occupy the violence-torn republic in January.[9] Muslim populations in some of the other republics were also showing signs of restlessness.

Even the Russian Republic—the heart of the Soviet Union, and the site of Moscow and the Kremlin— was demanding autonomy. Led by its president, Boris Yeltsin, it decreed that its laws took precedence over the laws of the Union of Soviet Socialist Republics. It was as though the state of New York had announced that its state laws overrode the Constitution of the United States. Other republics soon passed similar laws. Among them was the largest Soviet republic, the Ukraine.

And even while Mikhail Gorbachev was struggling to hold his restless union together, he also had to struggle to cure his desperately sick economy. *Perestroika* had been intended to bring economic relief, but if so, it was slow to act. By mid-1990, there had been few positive results for the Soviet economy, a fact that led to increasing dissatisfaction among the leadership and the people alike.

As the 1990s began, Gorbachev re-established himself in power. He had himself re-appointed to the two top jobs in the Soviet Union: President of the USSR, and Chairman of the Communist party. But as powerful as his position was, it was not secure. He was being pressured from all sides. At the 28th Communist Party Congress in Moscow, in the summer of 1990, many reformers rose to complain that Gorbachev's reforms were too few and too slow. Several of them, led by the increasingly popular Boris Yeltsin, actually walked out of the Congress—and out of the party. Such a thing had never happened before. At the same congress, conservatives (traditional Communists) were rising to complain that Gorbachev's reforms were moving too fast.

Most troubling of all to foreign observers were signs of growing discontent at all levels of the Soviet military. Ordinary soldiers, sent to Azerbaijan, were unhappy at having to use force against their own people. Meanwhile, according to U.S. Secretary of Defense Dick Cheney, there were reports that some top military officers were growing increasingly upset with both *perestroika* and *glasnost*. They wanted a return to the old ways of doing things. At the same time, many of the junior officers were pressing for stronger and faster reforms.[10]

Gorbachev seemed to jump back and forth between the forces of reform and the forces of Soviet conservatism. In one of the most shocking events in recent Soviet history, his longtime friend and ally Eduard Shevardnadze resigned as foreign minister. Shevardnadze had been one of the leading supporters of reform. In resigning, he warned that the Soviet Union was in danger of returning to dictatorship.

There is no way to tell what the future holds for the Soviet Union. It is possible that Gorbachev will ultimately succeed with his policies of slow reform, building an economically strong and politically much freer Soviet system. It is even possible that Yeltsin (or some other, more radical reformer) will come to power and subject the Soviet Union to something like the "shock therapy" that is being tried in Poland.

But other, much darker possibilities also exist. Total economic collapse is one of them. So is a military coup, whether led from the top by conservative generals, or by liberal officers from below. It is virtually certain that some republics will leave the Soviet Union. It is even possible that the USSR will break up altogether, splitting into fifteen or more separate countries.

In February 1991, Eduard Shevardnadze spoke publicly for the first time since his dramatic resignation. He used the occasion to issue another dark warning. The Soviet Union, he declared, was in danger of civil war.[11]

Whatever finally happens there, the ongoing upheaval in the Soviet Union is bound to have enormous effects around the world.

FACING THE FUTURE

So what *do* the events in Eastern Europe mean for the future? What will happen there? Will the newly independent and democratic governments of the region solve their countries' many problems, and embark on a new era of peace, freedom, and prosperity? Or will they sink into the repression and suffering of the past?

The final answers to these questions are years, maybe even decades, away. The Czechoslovakian Ambassador to the United States, Rita Klimova, may have described the bewildering prospects for the future best.

"It's all optimistic," she declared.

"But at the same time, if you get up close to it, and look at any partial aspect of it, it's very pessimistic.

"I mean," she concluded, "it's so difficult."

Difficult it will certainly be. But does that mean that we should look to the future with pessimism, because of the immensity of the problems challenging the nations of Eastern Europe? Or should we face the future with optimism, in light of the wonderful possibilities for peace and cooperation that have opened up so suddenly and unexpectedly?

The best answer, Ambassador Klimova suggests, may be "with both."[12]

SOURCE NOTES

THURSDAY, NOVEMBER 9, 1989

1. Hugh Sidey, "Present at the Construction," *Time,* Nov. 20, 1989, p. 33.

2. "Freedom!" *Time,* Nov. 20, 1989, p. 27.

3. Serge Schememann, "The Open Frontier; East Germans Flood the West, Most to Rejoice, Then Go Home; Kohl and Krenz Agree to Meet," in *The Collapse of Communism* by the correspondents of *The New York Times,* eds. Bernard Gwertzman and Michael T. Kaufman (New York: Times Books, 1990), p. 187.

4. Serge Schememann, "The Border Is Open; Joyous East Germans Pour Through Wall; Party Pledges Freedoms, and City Exults," in *Collapse of Communism,* p. 176.

5. Michael Meyer, Daniel Pedersen, and Karen Breslau, " 'Is It Possible?' " *Time,* Nov. 20, 1989, p. 27.

6. Ibid., p. 30.

CHAPTER ONE. PAST GLORIES

1. Historically, this region was commonly called Central Europe before the Soviet takeover. In this book, however, we will use the term Eastern Europe throughout in order to avoid confusion.

2. Paul Lendvai, *Eagles in Cobwebs: Nationalism and Communism in the Balkans* (Garden City, N.Y.: Doubleday, 1969), p. 33.

3. Edgar A. M. Sanderson and others, *The World's History and Its Makers* (New York: E. R. Du Mont, 1902), vol. 2, p. 147.

4. Those interested in Hungarian history before World War II can see Dominic G. Kosary, *A History of Hungary* (Arno, 1971).

5. Paul H. Beik and Laurence Lafore, *Modern Europe: A History since 1500* (New York: Holt, 1959), p. 156.

6. Sanderson, *The World's History*, p. 144.

7. For more details about Polish-Russian relations, see S. Konovalov, *Russo-Polish Relations: An Historical Survey* (Princeton, N.J.: Princeton University Press, 1945).

CHAPTER TWO. THE RUSSIAN BEAR

1. For more detailed information on this first real Russian state, see G. Vernadsky, *Kievan Russia* (New Haven, Conn.: Yale University Press, 1958).

2. Paul H. Beik and Laurence Lafore, *Modern Europe: A History Since 1500* (New York: Holt, 1959), p. 160.

3. For more on Russia's development as a European power, see B. H. Sumner, *Peter the Great and the Emergence of Russia* (New York: Teach Yourself History Series, 1951).

4. O. Halecki, *A History of Poland* (New York: Roy, 1976), p. 192.

5. Beik and Lafore, *Modern Europe*, p. 329.

6. Halecki, *History of Poland*, p. 220.

7. Jerzy Topolski, *An Outline History of Poland*, trans. Olgierd Wojtasiewicz (Warsaw: Interpress Publishers, 1986), p. 158.

8. Jorg K. Hoensch, *Modern History*, trans. Kim Traynor (London: Longman, 1988), p. 6.

9. Paul Ignotus, *Hungary* (New York: Praeger, 1972.) p. 57.

10. Ibid., p. 62.

11. Beik and Lafore, *Modern Europe*, p. 533.

CHAPTER THREE. THE END OF THE EMPIRES

1. Paul H. Beik and Laurence Lafore, *Modern Europe: A History since 1500* (New York: Holt, 1959), pp. 707–708.

2. Robert K. Massie, *Nicholas and Alexandra* (New York: Dell, 1967), p. 257.

3. For a detailed account of the actions and reactions, bluffs, and blunders, that led to World War I, see Barbara Tuchman, *The Guns of August* (New York: Macmillan, 1962).

4. Quoted by Massie, *Nicholas and Alexandra*, p. 104.

5. Beik and Lafore, *Modern Europe*, p. 770.

6. Karl Marx, *Capital—a Critique of Political Economy*, edited by Friederich Engels, revised and amplified by Ernest Untermann (New York: Modern Library, 1906).

7. For a more detailed explanation of socialism, Marxism, capitalism, and the difference between them, see Michael Kronenwetter, *Capitalism vs. Socialism* (New York: Franklin Watts, 1986).

8. John Reed, *Ten Days That Shook the World* (New York: Modern Library, 1935). The book was first published

in 1919. Reed, who was sympathetic to the Russian Revolution, died in the Soviet Union. He is the only American buried in a place of honor in the Kremlin.

9. Frederick G. Heymann, *Poland and Czechoslovakia* (Englewood Cliffs, N.J.: Prentice-Hall, 1966) pp. 132–133.

CHAPTER FOUR. A BRIEF MOMENT OF INDEPENDENCE

1. For an account of the murder of the czar and his family, see Robert K. Massie, *Nicholas and Alexandra* (New York: Dell, 1967), pp. 504–527.

2. For a detailed history of Hungary between the world wars, see Jorg K. Hoensch, *A History of Modern Hungary* (New York: Longman, 1988), pp. 85–145.

3. For a detailed account of Pilsudki's coup and the regime he established in Poland, see Richard M. Watts, *Bitter Glory: Poland and Its Fate 1918–1939* (New York: Simon and Schuster, 1979), particularly pp. 210–340.

4. Paul Lendvai, *Eagles in Cobwebs: Nationalism and Communism in the Balkans* (Garden City, N.Y.: Doubleday, 1969), p. 215.

5. Ibid., p. 212.

6. Ibid., p. 272.

7. For a biography of Masaryk, see Edward P. Newman, *Masaryk* (London: 1961). For a biography of Beneš, see E. B. Hitchcock, *Beneš, The Man and the Statesman* (London: 1940).

8. Frederick G. Heymann, *Poland and Czechoslovakia* (Englewood Cliffs, N.J.: Prentice-Hall, 1966), pp. 152–153.

9. Paul H. Beik and Laurence Lafore, *Modern Europe: A History since 1500* (New York: Holt, 1959), p. 860.

10. Anthony Read and David Fisher, *The Deadly Embrace: Hitler, Stalin, and the Nazi-Soviet Pact 1939–1941* (New York: W. W. Norton, 1988), p. 7.

11. Ibid., p. 419.

CHAPTER FIVE. AN "IRON" CURTAIN AND A "COLD" WAR

1. Richard N. Current, T. Harry Williams, and Frank Freidel, *American History: A Survey*, 4th ed. (New York: Knopf, 1975), p. 750.

2. Richard Worth, *Poland: The Threat to National Renewal* (New York: Franklin Watts, 1982), p. 9.

3. Jorg K. Hoensch, *A History of Modern Hungary 1867–1986*, trans. Kim Traynor (London: Longman, 1986) p. 149.

4. *Funk & Wagnalls New Encyclopedia* (New York: Funk & Wagnalls, 1986), vol. 22, p. 263.

5. Frederick G. Heymann, *Poland and Czechoslovakia* (Englewood Cliffs, N.J.: Prentice-Hall, 1966), p. 160.

6. Paul H. Beik and Laurence Lafore, *Modern Europe: A History since 1500* (New York: Holt, 1959), p. 894.

7. Hoensch, *Modern History*, pp. 181–183.

8. Paul Lendvai, *Eagles in Cobwebs: Nationalism and Communism in the Balkans* (Garden City, N.Y.: Doubleday, 1969), p. 284.

9. Lawrence Weschler, *Solidarity* (New York: Simon and Schuster, 1982), p. 14.

10. Jane Kramer, "Letter from Germany," *The New Yorker*, June 18, 1990, p. 64.

11. In his 1948 book *Fear, War, and the Bomb*, quoted in Current, Williams, and Friedel, *American History*, p. 755.

12. The words are from President Eisenhower's farewell address in 1961, quoted in Current, Williams, and Friedel, *American History*, p. 807.

CHAPTER SIX. "THE BREATH OF TRUTH"

1. For more on Khrushchev's attacks on Stalin, including his speech to the 20th Party Congress, see B. D. Wolfe, *Khrushchev and Stalin's Ghost*, (New York: Praeger, 1957).

2. Timothy Garton Ash, *The Polish Revolution: Solidarity* (New York: Charles Scribner's Sons, 1983), p. 8.

3. Clifton Daniel, ed. in chief, *Chronicle of the 20th Century* (Mount Kisco, NY: Chronicle, 1987), p. 790.

4. Ibid.

5. Jorg K. Hoensch, *Modern Hungary*, trans. Kim Traynor (London: Longman, 1988), p. 219.

6. *Britannica Book of the Year 1969* (Chicago: Encyclopaedia Britannica, 1969), p. 246.

7. Ambassador Rita Klimova, speaking at the U.S. Information Agency Conference on the Growth of Democracy, Washington, D.C., May 2, 1990.

8. *Britannica Book of the Year 1969*, p. 765.

9. Letter quoted in "People Watch," *USA Today*, May 4, 1990.

CHAPTER SEVEN. THE FOUNDATIONS FOR CHANGE

1. Timothy Garton Ash, *The Polish Revolution: Solidarity* (New York: Charles Scribner's Sons, 1983), p. 28.

2. Ibid., pp. 38–39.

3. Ibid., p. 260.

4. C. S. Manegold, and Scott Sullivan, "Freedom's Turn," *Newsweek*, August 28, 1989, p. 16.

5. A good chronology of the events in Poland leading up to the founding of Solidarity and the "state of war" declaration of December 1981, appears in Weschler, *Solidarity*, pp. 137–207.

6. Russell Watson, with Fred Coleman, "Life Without Lenin," in *Newsweek*, February 19, 1990, p. 21.

7. For a Western criticism of *perestroika*, see "Hurry, Doctor!" by Ed A. Hewitt and Richard Hornik, in *Time*, May 7, 1990, p. 84.

8. Parts, or all, of the sessions of this historic Congress were carried by both the CNN and C-SPAN cable networks.

CHAPTER EIGHT. THE PEACEFUL REVOLUTIONS OF 1989

1. Andrew Nagorski, "Will History Repeat Itself?" *Newsweek*, Aug. 28, 1989.

2. Bernard Gwertzman and Michael T. Kaufman, eds., *The Collapse of Communism* (New York: Times Books, 1990), p. 34.

3. Ibid., p. 122.

4. The closing chapters of this book deal mostly with events that took place while it was being written. Consequently, much of the information here was gathered from contemporary news reports. Among the sources most often consulted were *The New York Times, The Chicago Tribune, The Milwaukee Journal, The Milwaukee Sentinel*, national television broadcast news programs, CNN and C-SPAN cable television network news programs, and National Public Radio news broadcasts. Such information is cited only when it involves direct quotes or figures not commonly published in several of the sources.

5. Francis T. Miko, "East European Reform and U.S. Policy," a Congressional Research Service Issue Brief (Washington, D.C.: CRS, updated Mar. 2, 1990), p. 7.

6. Tim Cuprisin, "Hungarians Wait for Real Reform," *The Milwaukee Journal*, Mar. 6, 1990.

7. Paul Ignotus, *Hungary* (New York: Praeger, 1972), pp. 277–278.

8. A brief but very useful chronology of the main events of 1989 is available in "Upheaval in Eastern Europe," *Washington Post*, Dec. 23, 1989, p. A12.

9. Michael Meyer, "Days of the Whirlwind," *Newsweek*, Dec. 25, 1989, p. 26.

10. Miko, "East European Reform," p. 12.

11. William R. Doerner, "Freedom Train," *Time*, Oct. 16, 1989, p. 38.

12. Jane Kramer, "Letter from Germany," *The New Yorker*, June 18, 1990, p. 38.

13. Michael Meyer, "The Hollow Society," *Newsweek*, Feb. 26, 1990, p. 26.

14. Congressional Research Service/Library of Congress, "Germany's Future and U.S. Interests," a Congressional Research Service Issues Brief (Washington, D.C.: CRS, updated Feb. 23, 1990), p. 5.

15. Juan J. Walte, "E. Germans Vote for Unity," *USA Today*, Mar. 19, 1990.

16. "Czech Protest Ends in Bloody Melee," *Milwaukee Sentinel*, Nov. 18, 1989.

17. Meyer, "Days of the Whirlwind," p. 33.

18. Gwertzman and Kaufman, *Collapse of Communism*, p. 301.

19. "Czechoslovakia Ends Communist Monopoly," *Milwaukee Sentinel*, Nov. 30, 1989.

20. "2 Sister Groups Win Czech Election," *Milwaukee Sentinel*, June 11, 1990.

21. Miko, "East European Reform," p. 15.

22. "Upheaval in Eastern Europe," *Washington Post*, Dec. 23, 1989, p. A12.

23. Miko, "East European Reform," p. 15.

24. "Ex-Communists Pulling Ahead in Bulgaria," *USA Today*, June 18, 1990.

25. "Bulgarians Cheering After President Quits," *Chicago Tribune*, July 7, 1990.

26. "Bulgarian Protest Continues Despite Ouster of President," *New York Times*, July 8, 1990.

CHAPTER NINE. THE BLOODBATH IN ROMANIA

1. Bruce W. Nelan, "Slaughter in the Streets," *Time*, Jan. 1, 1990, pp. 34–37.

2. Francis T. Miko, "East European Reform and U.S. Policy," a Congressional Research Service Issue Brief (Washington, D.C.: CRS, updated Mar. 2, 1990), p. 14.

3. "Coroner: Romanian Massacre Never Happened," *Chicago Tribune*, Mar. 13, 1990.

4. Robert Cullen, "Report from Romania: Down with the Tyrant," *The New Yorker*, Apr. 2, 1990, p. 102.

5. Interview shown on "CNN News," Dec. 21, 1989.

6. Nelan, "Slaughter," p. 36.

7. "The End of the Affair," *Time*, Feb. 5, 1990, p. 47.

8. "Iliescu Elected to Lead Romania," *Chicago Tribune*, May 23, 1990.

9. "Romanian Soldiers Fire on Protestors," *Milwaukee Sentinel*, June 14, 1990; "Anti-Communist Protestors Return to Bucharest with Demands," *Chicago Tribune*, June 18, 1990.

10. "Romania Seeks Talks with Critics," *Chicago Tribune*, June 20, 1990.

CHAPTER TEN. THREE CHALLENGES FACING EASTERN EUROPE

1. John Greenwald, "New Kids on the Bloc," *Time*, July 2, 1990, p. 44.

2. "Radical Reform Set for Polish Economy," *Milwaukee Sentinel*, Dec. 18, 1989.

3. Ibid.

4. According to Alexander Cockburn, interviewed on "Nightline," ABC-TV, Jan. 5, 1990.

5. "Poland: The Morning After," "Frontline," WGBH Educational Television, broadcast over the Public Broadcasting System, Mar. 17, 1990.

6. Figures reported on "All Things Considered," National Public Radio, Mar. 21, 1990.

7. An unnamed Soviet economist, quoted by former U.S. ambassador Max Kampelman at the U.S. Information Agency Conference on the Growth of Democracy, Washington, D.C., May 2, 1990.

8. "Havel Gains Power and Popularity," *The Milwaukee Journal*, June 13, 1990.

9. Tom Matthews, Rod Nordland, and Carroll Bogert, "The Long Shadow," *Newsweek*, May 7, 1990, p. 44ff.

10. The figures and examples in this paragraph are taken from Frederick Painton, "Where the Sky Stays Dark," *Time*, May 28, 1990.

CHAPTER ELEVEN. THE POST–COLD WAR WORLD

1. "Berlin Events Signal Cold War Era's End," *USA Today*, Nov. 13, 1989.

2. Interviewed on CNN television, July 5, 1990.

3. R. C. Longworth and George de Lama, "NATO Allies to Soviets: Give Peace a Chance," *Chicago Tribune*, July 7, 1990.

4. John Stefany, "In Unity, Germans Still Seem Divided," *Milwaukee Journal*, Nov. 11, 1990.

5. Russell Watson and others, "The New Superpower," *Newsweek*, Feb. 26, 1990.

6. Frederick Painton, "What the Future Holds," *Time*, Dec. 18, 1989, p. 26.

7. For a discussion of the desire for independence in the Baltic republics, see Fred Coleman, "Until We Are Free Again" in *Newsweek*, Sept. 4, 1989, p. 28.

8. "Breaking from the Fold," *Newsweek,* Jan. 1, 1990, p. 33.

9. Bruce W. Nelan, Dean Fischer, and John Kohan, "Breaking Up Is Hard to Stop," *Time,* Jan. 15, 1990, p. 37.

10. Defense Secretary Cheney spoke about these reports in an interview on the Evans and Novak television program, cablecast on CNN, July 14, 1990.

11. National Public Radio (and other) news reports, Feb. 19, 1991.

12. Ambassador Klimova was speaking at the USIA Conference on the Growth of Democracy, held in Washington, D.C., May 2, 1990.

FOR FURTHER READING

The following list includes some of the more notable sources mentioned in the footnotes, as well as a selection of other books and articles of special interest.

BOOKS

Gwertzman, Bernard, and Michael T. Kaufman, eds. *The Collapse of Communism*. New York: Times Books, 1990. The events of 1989.

Hoensch, Jorg K. *Modern Hungary: 1867–1986*. Translated by Kim Traynor. London: Longman, 1988. A history.

Massie, Robert K. *Nicholas and Alexandra*. New York: Dell, 1967. Nicholas II and the end of the Russian Empire.

Read, Anthony, and David Fisher. *The Deadly Embrace: Hitler, Stalin, and the Nazi-Soviet Pact 1939–1941*. New York: W. W. Norton, 1988.

Reed, John. *Ten Days That Shook the World*. New York: Modern Library, 1935. The Russian Revolution.

Seton-Watson, H. *The East European Revolution*. 2nd ed. London: Methuen, 1951. The Soviet Union's takeover of Eastern Europe after World War II.

Watts, Richard M. *Bitter Glory: Poland and Its Fate 1918–1939*. New York: Simon and Schuster, 1979.

Weschler, Lawrence. *Solidarity*. New York: Simon and Schuster, 1982. Events leading up to the founding of the Solidarity trade union in Poland.

MAGAZINE ARTICLES AND OTHER
PUBLICATIONS

Cullen, Robert. "Report from Romania: Down with the Tyrant." *The New Yorker*, Apr. 2, 1990, p. 102. The overthrow of Ceausescu.

Elon, Amos. "Prague Autumn." *The New Yorker*, Jan. 2, 1990, p. 125. The velvet revolution in Czechoslovakia.

Kissinger, Henry A. "A Plan for Europe." *Newsweek*, June 18, 1990.

Kramer, Jane. "Letter from Germany." *The New Yorker*, June 18, 1990, p. 64. The question of reunification.

Matthews, Tom, Rod Nordland, and Carroll Bogert. "The Long Shadow," *Newsweek*, May 7, 1990, p. 44. Anti-Semitism in Eastern Europe.

Miko, Francis T. "East European Reform and U.S. Policy." A Congressional Research Service Issues Brief. Washington, D.C.: Congressional Research Service/Library of Congress, updated Mar. 2, 1990.

"People of the Year." *Newsweek*, Dec. 25, 1989. A *Newsweek* special report on the events in Eastern Europe in 1989, made up of several articles.

Shipler, David K. "Letter from Budapest." *The New Yorker*, Nov. 20, 1989, p. 74. The political and social conditions in Hungary prior to the first free elections there.

Weschler, Lawrence. "A Grand Experiment." *The New Yorker*, Nov. 13, 1989, p. 59. The situation in Poland as Solidarity began forming its first government.

INDEX

Agrarians, 53, 64

Albania, 9, 19, 73

Alexander, King of Serbia, 49

Alexander I, Czar, 31, 32

Allies, 12, 41, 65–66, 72–73

Anti-Semitism, 52, 55, 125

Antonescu, Ion, 63, 64

Austria, 22–23, 30–31, 33–34, 40, 56–57

Austria-Hungary, 34–35, 42

Axis powers, 63

Balkans, 39–42

Baltic republics, 9

Batthyany, Lajos, 33–34

Beneš, Eduard, 56, 58, 67

Berlin, 11–12, 64, 72

Berlin Wall: insert page 1, 11, 13–16, 104–105, 129–130, 133

Big Three nations, 66

Blackett, P. M. S., 73

Bloc, 71, 98–99

Bohemia, 18, 22, 48, 49

Bolsheviks, insert page 5; 46–47, 50

Borders: 18, 101, 102–103, 105, 133, 134

Boris III, King, 54

Bratianu, Ion, 54

Breshnev, Leonid, 83; doctrine of, 82–84, 108

Budapest, insert page 10; 79

Bulgaria, 9, 21, 40, 42, 53–54, 63, 67, 73, 108–111, 125, 127
Bulgars, 17, 19, 20, 24

Capitalism, 12–13, 46–47, 120–123
Carol, King, 63
Carol II, King, 54–55
Catherine the Great, insert page 4; 29
Catholics and Catholic church, 63, 70, 125
Ceauşescu, Nicolae, 71, 81, 113–116
Central Powers, 41
Charles II, King, 22
Cheney, Dick, 138
Chernobyl, 91–92, 94
Christian Democrats (Czechoslovakia), 108; (East Germany), 105–106, 133
Churchill, Winston, insert page 7; 62
Coalitions, 56, 66–67, 105–106
Cold War, 72–75, 129–131
Communism and communists: 63, 66–68, 72, 120–123
Communist Information Bureau (COMINFORM), 71, 77
Communist party: Bulgaria, 108–111; Czech-oslovakia, 107–108; East Germany, 12–13, 103–105; Hungary, 101–102; Poland, 69–70, 87–88; Romania, 114; Soviet, 50–51, 77, 90–92, 94–95, 138
Copsa Mica, insert page 15; 127
Corvinus, Matthias, 22
Council for Mutual Economic Assistance (COMECON), 71
Czechoslovakia, 9, insert page 11; 19, 48–49, 55–59, 67, 70, 73, 80–82, 106–108, 121, 125–126, 127

Das Kapital (Marx), 46
Demonstrations: insert page 16, 43–44, 80, 106–107, 110–118
Dubček, Alexander, 80–82, 84, 107

Eagles in Cobwebs (Landvai), 68
East Germany, 70, 102–106, 121
Economy, 69, 70, 91, 97–98, 100–101
Eisenhower, Dwight D., 74
Elections, 69, 98–99, 105–106, 109–110, 117–118

Emhke, Horst, 134
Environment, insert
    page 15; 126–127
Estonia, 26, 48, 60–61,
    136

Formula I auto race, 101
France, 41, 42, 73, 80
Francis Ferdinand,
    Arcduke, 40–41
Franz Joseph I, 34
Frederick II, King, insert
    page 4; 30

Gapon, Father George,
    44
Gaulle, Charles de, 80
Gerasimov, Gennady,
    131
German Democratic Re-
    public (GDR), 9, 12,
    72
German Federal Repub-
    lic, 12
Germany, 12–13, 42, 56–
    57, 62–63, 66, 132–136
Glasnost, 92–95
Glemp, Archbishop
    Jozef, 89
Gomulka, Wladislaw, 78
Gorbachev, Mikhail, in-
    sert page 12; 90–95,
    99, 104, 134–138
Gorgey, Arthur, 34
Great Britain, 31, 42, 73
Greens (East German),
    106

Gypsies, 63, 126
Gysi, Gregor, 105

Hapsburgs, 22, 34–35
Havel, Vaclav, insert
    page 13; 106, 107, 108,
    123, 124
Hitler, Adolf, 55–57, 60–
    61
Honecker, Erich, 103–
    105
Horthy, Miklós, 52
Hungarians and Hun-
    gary, 9, 21–23, 33–34,
    52, 63, 67–68, 73, 78–
    80, 100–103
Hunyadi, John, 22
Husak, Gustav, 82, 88

Iliescu, Ion, 116–118
Independence, insert
    page 16
Independent Student
    Association (Poland),
    98
Iron Curtain, insert page
    8; 62–75
Ivan I, Czar, 19
Ivan III, Grand Duke,
    insert page 3; 27–28

Jadwiga, Queen, 23
Jagiello, Grand Duke, 23
Jakes, Milos, 107
Jaruzelski, Wojciech,
    88–90
Jews, 53, 54, 63, 113–114

John Paul II, Pope, 85
John Sobieski, King. *See* Sobieski, John

Kadar, Janos, 79–80, 81, 102
Kaloyan, Czar 19
Károlyi, Count Mihály, 52
Kerensky, Alexander, 46
Khrushchev, Nikita, insert page 9, 13–14, 59, 77
Kirkpatrick, Jeane, 130
Kiszczak, Czeslaw, 99
Klimova, Rita, 82, 139–140
Kohl, Helmut, 134
Kossuth, Lajos, 34
Krenz, Egon, 104–105
Kun, Belá, 52

Ladislaus II, King, 22
Landvai, Paul, 68
Latvia, 26, 48, 60–61, 136
Lenin, V. I., 47–48
Lithuania, 26, 48, 60–61, 136–137
Louis II, King, 22
Louis the Great, King, 22
Lukanov, Andrei, 109–110
Lvov, Prince Georgi, 46

Magyars, 17, 19, 20, 21, 24, 33, 52

Maizière, Lothar de, 106, 133, 134
Marx, Karl, 46–47
Masaryk, Jan, 67
Masaryk, Tomáš, 49, 56, 67
Mazowiecki, Tadeusz, 99
Michael the Brave, 20–21
Michael, King, 64
Minorities, 57–58, 63, 113–114, 125–126
Mladenov, Petar, 109–111
Modrow, Hans, 105
Moise, Dominique, 135–136
Montenegro, 39, 40, 42
Moravia, 18–19, 21, 22, 48
Munich Agreement, 58
Muslims, 125, 137

Nagy, Imre, 79
National Peasants party, 54
National Salvation Front, 116–118
National Socialist party, 56
Nazi-Soviet Nonaggression Pact, insert page 6; 59–61
Nicholas I, Czar, insert page 5; 32–34
Nicholas II, Czar, 38, 41, 42–45

Nobel Prize, 96–97
North Atlantic Treaty Organization (NATO), 72, 73, 131, 133–134

Ottoman Empire, 19–20, 24

Peace of Kalowitz, 23
Peace of Tilsit, 31
Perestroika, 92–93
Peter the Great, insert page 3; 28–29
Peter I, King, 49
Peter III, King, 29
Pilsudski, Jozef, 53
Poland, 9, 23–24, 29–32, 42, 48, 53, 60, 62–63, 67, 73, 78, 85–90, 96–100, 122–123
Poland-Lithuania, 23–24, 27
Poniatowski, Stanislaw, 30
Prague, 49, 58, 106–107
Princip, Gavrilo, 49
Prussia, 23, 29–31

Reed, John, 47
Revolutions, 32–33, 42–48, 96–111
Ribbentrop, Joachim von, insert page 6
Romania, 9, insert page 14; 42, 54–55, 73, 112–118, 125

Rural Solidarity, 87, 98
Russia, 19, 23–27, 31–33, 38–39, 41–42, 47–48, 65. *See also* Soviet Union
Russia, republic of, 26, 137
Ruthenia, 49

Sakharov, Andrei, 84, 93, 94, 112–113
Serbs and Serbia, 17, 19, 35, 39, 40, 42
Shevardnadze, Eduard, 138, 139
Sigismund III, King, 23
Silesia, insert page 15; 18, 22, 49
Simeon I, King, 19
Slovaks and Slovakia, 17, 18, 47–49, 52, 81, 125–126
Sobieski, John, 24
Social Democrats: East German, 106; Hungarian, 68
Socialist Revolutionary party, 46
Solidarity, insert page 11; 68, 85–90, 96–100
Solzhenitsyn, Alexander, 93
Soviets, 45–46
Soviet Union, 9, 50–51, 60, 63–66, 68–71, 73, 79, 81–82, 90–95, 136–139. *See also* Russia

Stalin, Joseph, insert pages 6, 7; 50, 59, 77, 113

Stamboliski, Alexander, 53–54

Stanislaus II, King, 30

Stephen I, King, 21–22

Strikes, 86–88, 89, 98, 107

Sudetenland, 57–58

Suleiman the Magnificent, 22

Ten Days That Shook the World (Reed), 47

Tito, 82

Transylvania, 21, 22, 54

Treaty of Brest-Litovsk, 48

Tripartite Pact, 63

Turks and Turkey, 22–23, 73. *See also* Ottoman Empire

"2-plus-4 talks," 133

Ukrainians and Ukraine, 26, 53, 137

Ulyanov, Vladimir Ilyich (Lenin), 47

Union of Democratic Forces (Bulgaria), 110–111

Union of Soviet Socialist Republics. *See* Russia; Soviet Union

United States, 12–13, 72, 73, 80, 129, 132

Velvet Revolution, insert pages 2, 13; 106, 108

Vilnius, Lithuania, insert page 16

Wache, Angelika, 15

Walachia, 20

Walesa, Lech, insert page 11; 87–90, 96–97, 123, 124

Warsaw Pact, insert page 10; 73, 76, 82, 88, 108, 130–131

Weschler, Lawrence, 70

West Berlin, insert page 8

West Germany. *See* Germany

Wilhelm, Kaiser, 41

Wilson, Woodrow, 49

Wladyslaw II, King, 23

Wojtyla, Karol, 85

Workers' Guard, 102

World War I, 41, 44–48

World War II, 62–63

Yalta Agreement, 66

Yeltsin, Boris, 137, 138

Yugoslavia, 9, 71

Zagreb, Croatia, 49

Zapolya family, 22

Zhelov, Zhelyu, 111

Zhivkov, Todor, 109, 111